PENGUIN AN

THE ART OF RESILIENCE

Gauranga Das is a leadership and mindfulness coach based in Mumbai. A graduate of IIT Bombay, he found his calling to become a monk to best serve society. A member of ISKCON's Governing Body Commission, he is actively involved in enhancing leadership effectiveness and governance of temples and communities globally. He is dedicated to helping people transform their hearts, improve their attitudes, establish sustainable and spiritual communities, and drive positive change in society. A multifaceted spiritualist on a mission to create a value-based society, Gauranga Das is a mindful meditation expert, strategic character educationist, sustainability and climate change warrior, and social welfare catalyst.

Gauranga Das is director of ISKCON's Govardhan Ecovillage (GEV), founded by Radhanath Swami. The GEV, representing India, has won over thirty-four national and international awards, including the United Nations World Tourism Organization (UNWTO) Award in 2017 for its innovative model of 'Eco-Tourism as a Catalyst for Rural Development'. He has also strategized and led execution for GEV's synergistic solution for Sustainable Development Goals (SDGs) for Climate Change and enabled GEV's accreditation to multiple United Nations bodies like the ECOSOC, UNEP and UNCCD. The Indian Green Building Council (IGBC) has recognized him as an IGBC Fellow for his contribution to the green building movement.

He sits on the board of the Govardhan School of Public Leadership, an institution that prepares students for the civil services exam. He has led several youth empowerment initiatives while successfully inculcating clarity in purpose, purity in character and compassion in relationships in thousands of youths globally. He is also the administrative director of Bhaktivedanta Research Centre (BRC), an initiative of ISKCON to connect working professionals, housewives and students to the academic study of philosophy, create libraries of Vedic literatures and manuscripts, and facilitate MA and PhD programmes in philosophy.

ADVANCE PRAISE FOR THE BOOK

'The parameters of success for the global business community have evolved over time with changing business paradigms, advent of technology, and, most importantly, customer expectations and behaviour. As we still figure this out, this book of yoga stories offers a perspective where certain parameters don't change at all; rather, they define success in life.'—Ajay Piramal, chairman, Piramal Group

'Wealth creation is a function of success for modern-day entrepreneurs. In the quest to create external value, some of them lose the plot and fail to create value within. This book of yoga stories has much to offer for them to help create value holistically.'—Ashish Chauhan, MD and CEO, Bombay Stock Exchange

'Gauranga Das's lessons will transform your heart. When you apply them in your life, you will experience the stillness of mind to make better decisions and move in the right direction. His life and teachings have impacted me deeply, and now they're available to you in this book.'—Jay Shetty, *New York Times* bestselling author, podcaster, storyteller and philanthropist

'Technology has been able to connect people externally but there's a missing link within. Take a dip into this pond of yoga stories as Gauranga Das guides you to reconnect from within.'—Vijay P. Bhatkar, architect, Param Supercomputers, and Padma Bhushan and Padma Shri awardee

'In this day and age, one cannot deny the need for compassion, wisdom, strength, will power and, most importantly, humanity. Gauranga Das's book, *The Art of Resilience*, based on the values and teachings of Srimad Bhagavad Gita, is a very thoughtful way to not only share impactful and inspiring stories, but also instil humanitarian values through other people's life experiences. There's something for every reader in these stories, and I'd like to wish Gauranga Das the very best in his journey ahead. Atmanamaste!'—Shilpa Shetty Kundra, actor, entrepreneur, mindful yogi, wellness influencer

'Gauranga Das Prabhu has been my personal inspiration on giving moral values through stories. His storytelling style is unique, simple and profound. Every story invokes a new dimension of thinking. The eternal wisdom that these stories impart will change you forever. Read each story and tell it to someone else. These are meant to be shared with all. I would like to thank Gauranga Prabhu for bringing these gems of wisdoms to every spiritual seeker and common man.'—Radhakrishnan Pillai, author, and director, Chanakya International Institute of Leadership Studies (CIILS)

'In this book, Gauranga Das ji evokes the idea of mindful behavioural practice, by drawing lessons from ancient Indian literatures, which are timeless and timely, especially since the world is still reeling under a global pandemic. The lessons are conveyed through beautiful stories and Sanskrit verses. An excellent book that should be read by everyone.'—Kal Raman, chief digital officer, Samsung America

'We are often told that change is the only constant, no matter what the set-up. This makes us wonder if there is something at all that is constant. Gauranga Das ji in this book reveals the other constants that are well within us and over which we have unlimited control. Swim into this ocean of knowledge and inspiration.'—Vivek Bindra, founder and CEO, Bada Business, entrepreneur, and business coach

'An inward journey that is at once pragmatic and profound, *The Art of Resilience* is an eternal guide for those seeking solution and solace. Written with both sensitivity and authority, Gauranga Prabhu has authored a masterly book.'—Shuvendu Sen, bestselling author and recipient of the United States Nautilus Award

The Art of
RESILIENCE

40 STORIES *to* uplift the mind
and transform the heart

GAURANGA DAS

PENGUIN
ANANDA

An imprint of Penguin Random House

PENGUIN ANANDA

USA | Canada | UK | Ireland | Australia
New Zealand | India | South Africa | China

Penguin Ananda is part of the Penguin Random House group of companies
whose addresses can be found at global.penguinrandomhouse.com

Published by Penguin Random House India Pvt. Ltd
7th Floor, Infinity Tower C, DLF Cyber City,
Gurgaon 122 002, Haryana, India

Penguin
Random House
India

This edition published in Penguin Ananda by Penguin Random House India 2021

Copyright © Gauranga Das 2021

All rights reserved

10 9 8 7 6 5 4 3 2 1

The views and opinions expressed in this book are the author's own and the
facts are as reported by him which have been verified to the extent possible,
and the publishers are not in any way liable for the same.

These stories have been told since time immemorial in different ways
by different seekers. The author has retold them in a different context for
the modern generation so they can benefit from their timeless wisdom.

ISBN 9780143452737

Typeset in Adobe Caslon Pro by Manipal Technologies Limited, Manipal

All the proceeds from the sale of this book will be directly utilized
for the Govardhan Annakshetra food distribution programme.

This book is sold subject to the condition that it shall not, by way of trade
or otherwise, be lent, resold, hired out, or otherwise circulated without the
publisher's prior consent in any form of binding or cover other than that in
which it is published and without a similar condition including this condition
being imposed on the subsequent purchaser.

www.penguin.co.in

To the three people who changed my life forever—
His Divine Grace A.C. Bhaktivedanta Swami Srila Prabhupada,
the founder Acharya of ISKCON;
His Holiness Radhanath Swami, my spiritual master; and
His Holiness Bhaktirasamrita Swami, my first spiritual mentor.

'Resilience and tenacity are central to India's ethos. In our glorious history, we have faced moments that may have slowed us but never crushed our spirit. We have bounced back again and gone on to do spectacular things. That is why our civilization stands tall.'—Narendra Modi, prime minister of India, in an address to ISRO scientists in September 2019

'Where there is resolve and resilience, resources come naturally.'—Narendra Modi at the 18th Convocation of Tezpur University, held in Assam on 22 January 2021

Contents

Introduction   xiii

1. The Balm of Forgiveness   1
   Human Quality: Self-Identity

2. The Instruments Should Be Humble   7
   Human Quality: Modesty

3. An Empty Boat   13
   Human Quality: Mind Control

4. The Secret of Meditation   19
   Human Quality: Tolerance

5. Quality Determines Success   26
   Human Quality: Gratitude

6. Faith in the Supreme Well-Wisher   31
   Human Quality: Faith

7. The Tree and the Carpenter Team   38
   Human Quality: Maturity

8. Krishna as the Centre of Our Life   45
    Human Quality: Devotion

9. The Mystery of Blessings   53
    Human Quality: Blessings

10. Team Spirit   59
    Human Quality: Association

11. The Conqueror Conquered   64
    Human Quality: Spirituality

12. The Mystery of the Chessboard   70
    Human Quality: Self-Improvement

13. Overcoming an Inferiority Complex   75
    Human Quality: Inferiority

14. Honesty Wins   80
    Human Quality: Honesty

15. Gossip Passes the Karma too   86
    Human Quality: Verbal Austerity

16. Do You Want to Become the Most Powerful?   92
    Human Quality: Satisfaction

17. Leadership Means Integrity   99
    Human Quality: Integrity

18. The Gift of Patience   104
    Human Quality: Sense Control

19. Fool's Friendship Is Fatal   111
    Human Quality: Self-Discipline

20. Comforting the Distressed   118
    Human Quality: Service Attitude

21. Getting Out of the Prison   124
    Human Quality: Repentance

22. The Cup or the Juice   131
    Human Quality: Detachment

23. Monkeys in the Well   138
    Human Quality: Cooperation

24. Power of Hearing   144
    Human Quality: Self-Transformation

25. How to Invest Time Properly   151
    Human Quality: Prioritization

26. Mystery of Destiny   159
    Human Quality: Transcendence

27. Conquering Pride   167
    Human Quality: Humility

28. Thirst Dilemma   175
    Human Quality: Giving

29. Palace or Guest House   183
    Human Quality: Detachment

30. The Coconut Story   192
    Human Quality: Wisdom

31. Provocations and Self-Control   200
    Human Quality: Self-Control

32. Cheating through Profit   209
    Human Quality: Mindfulness

33. Selfishness Is Self-Destructive   218
    Human Quality: Friendship

34. Power of Obedience   226
    Human Quality: Submissiveness

35. Funny Justice   235
    Human Quality: Self-Control

36. Service in Anticipation   243
    Human Quality: Service Attitude

37. Two Precious Jewels   251
    Human Quality: Integrity

38. When to Fight, When to Submit   259
    Human Quality: Seeking Shelter

39. Move from Comfort Zone to Effort Zone   268
    Human Quality: Equality

40. Who Can Escape the Chase?   279
    Human Quality: Humaneness

Acknowledgements   289

Introduction

I have been a monk for over twenty-seven years. When I tell people I am a monk, the image they seem to conjure up is that of a man of the cloth who meditates in tranquillity for hours on end. In part, they are correct. I do meditate for over two hours daily, chanting the Hare Krishna maha mantra with focused attention. However, the remaining twenty-two hours are filled with a different flavour of tranquillity. They are filled with being involved in a plethora of spiritually inspired selfless service.

For one of these services, I travel the world to talk about the Vedic literatures I have studied intensively and based my life on. Specifically the three main literatures, including the famous *Bhagavad Gita As It Is,* heralded as the main source of wisdom for Hindus globally and from which most of the lessons of this book are derived. It is sometimes cited as the textbook of God. The second book is the *Srimad Bhagavatam*, an extensive 18,000 verse treatise on God by Veda Vyasa, translated into English by A.C. Bhaktivedanta Swami Prabhupada. This book is sometimes cited as the biography of God. The third book is the *Chaitanya Charitamrita*, the life and teachings of Sri Chaitanya

Mahaprabhu, a fifteenth-century incarnation of God. This book is sometimes cited as the diary of God. Each book has its place in society; each adding layers of truths about the Supreme, just as children are taught about the rules of mathematics as they advance from one grade to another.

From my experience speaking around the world, I have realized that for many, it is easier to absorb the truths of literatures like the *Bhagavad Gita As It Is* when it is supplemented by stories. Stories give a context and application to truth. Stories help us imagine ourselves in the characters' roles and apply the lesson that they are learning in our own lives. It is easier to learn the lesson of 'being grateful' in the context of a story rather than from being told to simply 'be grateful'. There is no doubt that ancient Vedic heavyweight literatures such as the Mahabharata and the Ramayana are so popular because they teach universal truths through stories unparalleled in their excitement, engagement and depth.

The Art of Resilience is the first book in a three-part series. It takes the same principle of telling enamouring cultural stories and bringing to light universal truths that are found within them. As stated, I have primarily used *Bhagavad Gita As It Is* and other Vedic literatures to bring out the lessons of these stories. The main topics include, understanding the spiritual nature of the human condition (*atma*), the components of the world around us (*prakriti*), the influence time has on our life (*kala*), how our actions in the past created our present and how our present actions can affect our future (*karma*) and the influence of the Supreme control over everything and everyone (*isvara*).

This book is for those searching to build resilience in the face of adversity, trauma, tragedy or significant sources of stress, such as family and relationship problems, serious health problems or workplace and financial stresses. What makes this book different is that the timeless principles explaining the stories are based on authentic, timeless Vedic wisdom. They address issues at a level far beyond the popular and well-trodden path of self-help. These principles are also eternal and time-tested, and can enrich our lives if we follow them sincerely. I do not claim to be the author of these ideas. Indeed, these ideas originate in Krishna Himself and have been taught by several spiritual teachers like H.D.G. Srila A.C. Bhaktivedanta Swami Prabhupada, the Founder Acharya of the International Society of Krishna Consciousness (ISKCON), to those committed to understanding Him in succession. I am simply an instrument to help you find relevance, utility and joyful transformation through these topics and doing my utmost to show you how they can be applied to the real world.

ONE

The Balm of Forgiveness

Human Quality: Self-Identity

Shakti was a tradesman who travelled extensively for work. Being away from his hometown and family, he often felt lonely. Often, he would be so engrossed in his work that he would skip meals, making him stressed. Not knowing how to deal with this stress, he would turn to alcohol, movies, spectator sports and endless Internet browsing for his enjoyment. Worst of all, his late-night Internet addiction made him lose sleep, health and mental clarity.

Once, Shakti was travelling to a new town on a work trip. He had shortlisted the prospective businesses he was going to visit in the morning and was positive that he would make a sale. Driven by habit, Shakti stayed up till late in the night scrolling through unscrupulous websites on the Internet. The next morning, Shakti snoozed his alarm several times and before he realized it, he had woken up late. He had to skip breakfast to keep the first appointment.

By the evening, Shakti was exhausted. It was almost 6 p.m., he hadn't eaten all day and none of his deals had materialized. Feeling depressed, Shakti went to a roadside eatery for dinner.

While he was having his meal, a few travelling monks walked past the restaurant. It was an unusual sight to witness; usually you only saw monks in temples. Quickly slurping the rest of his daal and wiping his mouth with the sleeve of his coat, Shakti rushed to follow the sound of their devotional singing. As he reached the place, he saw a few dozen monks sitting on the floor with their leader seated on a raised platform under a banyan tree. The guru was speaking on the intrinsic nature of the material and spiritual realities.

'There is more to you than the physiological and psychological aspects of your existence. You are not just your body and you are neither your mind alone. The Bhagavad Gita explains that beyond the physical and the psychological is the spiritual dimension. The "spiritual you" or the soul is the real you. And this soul is "sat-chid-ananda" in nature. That means this eternal part of you is full of knowledge and bliss, in its natural spiritual state.'

While the disciples heard the guru's descriptions from the Gita with keen interest, waves of rage ran through Shakti's mind. 'I have not experienced any of this pleasure he speaks about,' he thought. 'There is no such thing as eternal happiness.' Though unaware of it, Shakti's late-night escapes from life's hard knocks to the virtual world of Internet obscenity had slowly turned him brutish. Not knowing how to respond, whether to protest or seek a clarification, Shakti approached the guru. In great anger, he spat on the old man's face. Shocked, the disciples instantly rose to retaliate, but the guru immediately asked them to sit down peacefully.

'Go on . . .' the gentle guru politely encouraged his assailant. Boiling over with anger and having lost all mental composure, Shakti's unhealthy mind disapproved of the guru's words. He spat at the guru's face again with deep indignation as his bloodshot eyes surveyed the guru's facial expression. With chaotic uproar, the disciples rose again. The guru intervened again and commanded silence. Again, turning calmly to his attacker, the guru repeated, 'What is it? Go on . . .' Infuriated, speechless and breathing heavily, Shakti stomped away without a word.

With Shakti gone, the broken-hearted followers turned to their guru saying, 'This man has no regard for the defenceless noble saints. He insulted you gravely and you stopped us, but we are going to deal with him.'

The guru replied, 'I command you not to harm him. Stay calm; this man had something to say, but could not express himself as he was choked up by his emotions. Therefore, although wanting to speak, he could not say a thing. And so when I said, "Go on . . .", I was encouraging him to speak and clear his mind. Don't be surprised if he comes again.'

As predicted, the next evening, Shakti returned to where he met the guru, dishevelled and with an uneasy air about him. The disciples became alarmed at his presence, ready to confront him as he approached the guru.

Looking at the guru with soft eyes and quivering lips, Shakti positioned himself. In a moment he fell at the feet of the guru and started crying, sobbing uncontrollably while holding the guru's feet. The guru raised Shakti, looked at him and encouraged him as before, 'Go on . . .' Shakti continued crying inconsolably. The guru gave him time to collect himself and after a few minutes said again, 'Go on . . .' Shakti kept crying with his face in his hands.

The guru then said, 'You are a man of powerful emotions with a lot to share. Somehow, the words you seek are lost to you. It takes two things to grow: making the right decision and support to follow that decision. You can win over your mind by the correct use of your intelligence.'

Hearing these words, still sobbing, Shakti replied, 'Please forgive me for what I did to you yesterday.'

The guru exclaimed, 'Yesterday! "Yesterday" was yesterday! Today is "today"! Time is like a river. You can't bathe in the same river twice since the water passes on. Similarly, the body and the mind change constantly. It is not worth lamenting the past.

'The only thing which remains unchanged from yesterday and yesteryear is the eternal soul within. That sense of your "I-ness" never changes. Better do something for that part of you which is always going to stay with you, which is the real you! Let us try to realize our eternal spiritual nature to develop as noble individuals. Then you will be able to remain fixed, unmoved by the disturbing dualities of your mind, despite the challenges life gives you,' concluded the guru with a reassuring smile.

kāṭhinyam giriṣu sadā mṛdulatā salile dhruva prabhā sūrye
Vairamasajjanahṛdaye sajjanhṛdaye punhh kṣāntiḥ
(Mahāsubhāṣitasaṃgraha 9373)

This wisdom presents a comparison between the temperaments of mean-minded and noble-minded people. Just as the mountains exemplify firmness, water illustrates mildness and the sun symbolizes brightness, similarly, mean-minded persons engage in inimical thoughts and deeds. In contrast, the noble-hearted always exemplify tolerance and patience.

DO YOU EXPERIENCE DISTURBING THOUGHTS?

Ancient yoga texts explain that the spirit soul experiences the material world with the help of the mind and the senses. Any experience perceived by the senses is stored in the subconscious mind as a '*samskaar*'. Therefore, whatever we feed our minds through our various senses builds new samskaars or enforces the ones that already exist in our subconscious mind. For example, we may scroll for hours on social media unaware of the subtle effect this is having on our subconscious mind.

These samskaars or impressions carry a bioenergy in the brain and drive our behaviour as automated responses later. It is something like building a neurological habit akin to muscle memory that athletes build by repeated exposure to the same practice.

By repeatedly being exposed to or succumbing to disturbing thoughts, we strengthen their grip on us. 'Stuck thoughts' are unwanted intrusive thoughts that often focus on sexual, violent or socially unacceptable images. Fearful of committing such acts as pictured by the mind, one experiences anxiety, decreased determination and lack of self-control, as Shakti did.

HOW DO WE REDUCE OUR DISTURBING THOUGHTS?

To begin the cleansing of your psyche, check your exposure to provocative images and experiences that trigger you negatively.

When disturbing thoughts inevitably appear in your mind, neglect them and do not give them much attention. The yogic practice recommends that to eliminate disturbing thoughts from the mind, we must think of an opposite positive thought, as soon as it appears within our mind's eye.

Meditating on the opposite positive thought is not limited to just thinking rationally and superficially about it forcefully. It means meditating on it (*chintan*), by going into the depths of our minds (*manan*), living in the opposite positive thought (*bhaavana*) and acting out the positive thought (*sevanam*).

Only by cultivating a strong sentiment and emotional connection to the positive thoughts, can we start eradicating the latent negative samskaars, which are the fixed, habitual and enslaving negative impressions in our minds.

The path of *bhakti-yoga* given in the Gita is designed to give wholesome positive engagements to all aspects of ourselves; our real self (the *atma*), our senses (*indriya*), our mind (*manas*), our intelligence (*buddhi*) and the ego impression (*ahankaar*). Bhakti-yoga is a positive path in which we can actively reduce our negative samskaars, by acting in a way that is beneficial for our real selves.

TWO

The Instruments Should Be Humble

Human Quality: Modesty

King Jyotinaabh had a taste for excellence. Although an accomplished statesman, he found himself becoming envious of his commander-in-chief, Yuyutsu. Both of them were expert archers, but Yuyutsu's precision and speed were next to none. The king had tried to suppress his envy of the great archer, but to no avail. He felt especially uneasy when citizens expressed their awe of Yuyutsu's skill at public events.

Having acknowledged Yuyutsu's contribution to the state and wanting to develop a deeper sense of appreciation for him, King Jyotinaabh decided to publicly award him. After discussions with his council of ministers, it was decided that during the upcoming annual parade, Yuyutsu would be awarded the highest military decoration for his valour, courageous actions and self-sacrificing spirit.

The annual parade was an elaborate event. It saw the heads of state, members of the social elite and thousands of citizens come together to celebrate the achievements of the kingdom. After the various cultural presentations, soldiers exhibited their military abilities—strength, fighting abilities and weapon skills.

During the parade, as a sign of respect, Yuyutsu led the armed forces in a salute to the king and the royal throne. The crowd, however, was waiting for Yuyutsu to display his unmatched skill in great anticipation. For his first demonstration, Yuyutsu galloped blindfolded on a horse while hitting targets with his bow and arrows. He next demonstrated his precision by way of underwater targets and his might fighting alone with a dozen armed men. Thwarting a 360-degree attack by spinning on a chariot wheel while releasing arrows like beams of torchlight, Yuyutsu left the audience spellbound and in awe.

After his presentation, the brass horns blared to signify an announcement from the speaker of the royal court. He stepped up to the podium and announced that King Jyotinaabh would be felicitating the most accomplished in the kingdom. Yuyutsu was caught by surprise as his name was declared for the highest gallantry award.

Wanting to understand Yuyutsu's heart, the king had asked his ministers to maintain complete secrecy about the ceremony. The king wanted to see Yuyutsu's real reaction to the honour bestowed upon him. With thundering applause around the arena, the award was placed on Yuyutsu's broad chest by a grave and appreciative king. Yuyutsu was asked to give a speech in acknowledgement of his award. The king watched closely to catch any glimpse of pride swell up in the heart of Yuyutsu.

An unprepared Yuyutsu then spoke, 'Thank you for the honour, your highness. It is the highest privilege for me to serve my country and a noble king like you. Assembled friends, I once saw a saint entering one of our metro cities.

He was riding a donkey. People were throwing flowers upon him to welcome him. But as these flowers were being thrown upon the saint, I saw that the donkey started braying. The braying continued while the donkey walked through the main street of the city. I remember how the saint looked neither impressed by the honour being given to him nor embarrassed by the donkey's comical antics.'

The crowd and the celebrities looked at Yuyutsu with interest as he continued his speech.

'Afterwards, I approached the saint and asked him what he was thinking when he was being showered with flowers. The saint humbly told me that he saw himself as an insignificant instrument in the hands of God. He was grateful to all the people of the city who had gathered there so graciously, only in appreciation of God's grace flowing through him. However, he said that he had no personal qualification to receive such honour. The saint said that it was only due to God's giving him the privilege to serve Him that he was being offered all this respect. And he said that it was his duty to pass God's grace to all His creation and all the glorification back to God.'

Ending his narrative, Yuyutsu said, 'Today, I too have been honoured by our king. There is no personal merit to me, but it is only by his grace that I can be of service to you all. I am simply an instrument in King Jyotinaabh's hands. He personally trained me and he's my inspiration in life. His support, wise counsel and definitive leadership have been the foundation of my success.'

Turning to his king, the ace archer spoke further, 'My lord, I have always wondered why the donkey was braying as the flowers were being showered on the saint. I understand today that the donkey was perhaps thinking, "At last, these people have finally realized my true glory! They are thus worshipping and respecting me by showering these flowers."'

With his hand on his heart and bowing his head towards the king, Yuyutsu concluded, 'In the spirit of that saint, I acknowledge this award as the grace and affection of my king, without whose exemplary leadership I would only end up thinking like that donkey.'

The king stood up applauding as Yuyutsu concluded his speech. The last twinges of envy in the king's heart melted away in affection for this superior warrior and humble individual.

> *vidyā vivādayā dhanam madāya,*
> *śaktiḥ pareṣāṁ parpīḍnāya*
> *khalasya sādho viparītaṁ etad,*
> *jñānāya dānāya ca rakṣaṇāya*

This verse describes that for the wicked, knowledge is only a tool for arguments, their wealth is only a means to blow up their ego and the power they possess is simply wasted in troubling others. But the opposite is true for those with a noble heart. The virtuous put their knowledge to good use to benefit others, their wealth supports noble causes, and their power and influence are used to protect the weak or vulnerable without discrimination or bias.

HOW CAN WE CULTIVATE NOBILITY OF HEART?

IT STARTS WITH GRATITUDE

Who can claim to have planned or created their own sense faculties like seeing and smelling? Who can claim to be the cause behind the facilities and resources of nature? No one was born a mathematician or a musician. Whether a chance-based evolutionary biologist or a mystery-driven religious creationist, it's easy to see we are dependent on others.

Nature's gifts are not resources designed by man, but are the grace of God. It helps us grow when we acknowledge how we are individually graced and guided for what we need and possess in our lives. Therefore, the gifts of our basic abilities—to speak, to hear, to move, to laugh, or the gifts of our higher sense—to think, to use logic or even to love, everything calls for gratitude.

GRATITUDE GROWS INTO SERVICE

The Gita explains how to make the most of our relationships. A sense of appreciation and respect are the symptoms of a grateful heart. The sprouting of gratitude begins to fructify in reciprocal service to those who have benefited us. Furthermore, gratitude graduates in selfless service to others without gain or obligation in mind.

SERVICE ENTAILS RESPONSIBILITY

Service to others helps us rise above our own self-gratification and petty selfishness. Service is gratitude put into action. Obliging ourselves for the benefit of others helps us develop responsible attitudes in life. It expands our vision from ourselves to others. It gives us insights on how our actions impact not just ourselves, but others around us. When we become responsible towards ourselves, towards each other and towards our planet, we inadvertently become more considerate and less destructive. This starts with gratitude.

HOW CAN WE DEAL WITH OUR ENVY OF THOSE WHO ARE BETTER THAN US?

Acknowledge their greater ability to develop better skills.

Appreciate them in person for their dedication to reach excellence.

Award their contribution publicly. A genuine public thank you can help clear the heart of envy.

Affectionately see their talents as a gift from God, utilized for serving Him better.

WHY ARE SOME PEOPLE MORE GIFTED THAN OTHERS?

Our talents and abilities or lack thereof are all controlled by the Law of Karma. Every action has an equal and opposite reaction or 'We reap what we sow'. The universe is a university; it is teaching us through reward and punishment that we are never alone in our success or failures. Instead of allowing envy for others to creep in, one need only work on oneself in humble partnership with God.

THREE

An Empty Boat

Human Quality: Mind Control

Looking for a solution for his sleepless nights and anxiety attacks, a young man learnt that yoga and meditation can help to pacify the mind. He began to explore the various methods for learning yoga and meditation. Experimenting with this science, he cherry-picked different principles from different schools of yoga. He was more like a spiritual shopper than a spiritual seeker.

After going here and there, he finally stumbled across a group of bhakti-yogis and was deeply impressed by the depth of their practical knowledge of yoga philosophy. He found out that they were students of a very experienced yoga master representing an authentic traditional lineage in India. Setting aside time for his well-being, he took a two-month sabbatical to master the basics of yoga practice and learn about the science of the self.

'Yoga literature explains that there are four levels of sleep. To access deeper tranquillity, one has to begin by mastering the mind and learning to control its unrestricted wanderings. The very first principle of yoga is to understand that you are not your body. The real you is even beyond your own thoughts and feelings. The true self lies within the body, but is beyond the mind and the intelligence,' explained the guru in his first lecture to the new attendees at his ashram.

'In the Gita, it is explained at great length how the mind is the cause of bondage and, at the same time, is the cause of freedom. A mind that is controlled is one's best friend, but an uncontrolled mind is the greatest enemy of the person,' the guru elaborated, quoting texts from the sixth chapter of the Gita.

Soon, in the company of saintly people, the young apprentice quickly found some peace and relief. But while seeking peace of mind, he was quick to chastise his peers who he felt disturbed his practice. Tranquillity was thus forced to be silence and anybody who became the cause of disturbing it, was told off by the novice meditator.

A few days of this military-like regime later, the young man concluded that the ashram was too crowded to practise mind control. He thought of going to a lonely, undisturbed place. Contemplating thus, one fine day he went to a serene lake and set off to the middle in a rowing boat. After stationing the boat there, he sat comfortably and started his meditation.

Observing the complete silence of his surroundings, he experienced the stillness of the ambience and observed his thoughts flowing within his mind. 'Yes! I am finally aware of my own thoughts, like a third person viewing the movie of his own life being played on a projection screen. These thoughts are coming and going of their own accord and I am simply a witness without implicating myself with the working of these mental longings. I see how I am the observer of my thoughts and not my thoughts!'

As he was going deeper into his meditation, he suddenly experienced a strong jerk. All his meditative focus immediately left. In great anger, his instant thoughts were, 'Good Lord! I came all the way to this quiet lake. Who is disturbing me here?'

As he opened his eyes and looked around, he found nobody there. He realized that, flowing down the river stream, an empty boat had hit his own. Who could he hold responsible for the cause of anger and disturbance in him now? This triggered deeper thoughtfulness in him.

'The cause of negative emotions is something within us, not outside us.' These words of the guru now made sense. He realized that anger was already within him. The boat simply became an instrument to trigger that anger.

Therefore, taught by providence, the apprentice decided not to search for the cause of disturbance outside of himself. He was beginning to mature in his understanding. He decided to work on his inner self rather than trying to correct and control everything around him. He resolved that in future, whenever he would go through provoking situations, he would look at his provocateurs as boats colliding with him carried by the waves of time.

At the same time, he remembered what the guru had mentioned in another talk, 'Spirituality is not about suppressing disturbing thoughts, rather it is about transcending disturbing thoughts by filling our consciousness with better thoughts. Bhakti-yoga is the process of filling our consciousness with thoughts of the all-attractive, all-powerful, all-loving supreme person, God or Krishna.'

> *nāyaṁ jano me sukha-duḥkha-hetur*
> *na devatātmā graha-karma-kālāḥ*
> *manaḥ paraṁ kāraṇam āmananti*
> *saṁsāra-cakraṁ parivartayed yat*
> (Srimad Bhagavatam 11.23.42)

This insightful verse from the *Srimad Bhagavatam* presents a deep analysis of who is to blame for our suffering. When something goes wrong:

- We should not accuse other people; they are only the instrumental cause in the matter.
- We should not accuse demigods like Chandra (the moon god); they are only the remote cause.
- Nor should we accuse astral bodies like the malefic planets—Rahu or Saturn; they are only influencers.
- Karma too is not to be blamed; it is only the resultant energy of our own past actions.
- Time is not to be accused either; as providence, it is only the witness.
- But the mind alone is said to be the main culprit.

Being the thinking, feeling and willing initiator, and responding to all our experiences, our mind is the only cause for whatever happens to us in this world.

As spiritual beings with material bodies, we give away our control by misidentifying ourselves with the physical (the body), the psychological (the mind) and the intellectual (the intelligence) layers of our existence. Thus, by properly understanding and realizing our spiritual nature, which is different from these other three layers, we can better use the body, the mind and the intelligence to win over all negativity.

WHAT IS THE MIND?

The mind is like an inner screen that is meant to display inputs from the senses for our souls to perceive and process. Thus, the mind is like a window to the outer world for us to operate in it.

WHY BE CAREFUL OF THE MIND?

The mind can *sedate* us away from our responsibilities, to live 'mindlessly' and waste time. It is only the mind that makes doable appear as difficult and useless appear as important. Furthermore, the mind *seduces* us into doing unwanted or regrettable things by painting an irresistible picture of pleasure. Once the indulgence is over and it turns out to be disappointing or trouble-inducing, the mind *scolds* us for having acted so stupidly. How many incidents can you remember when your own mind tipped you, tricked you, tripped you and then trapped you?

HOW DO WE CONTROL THE MIND?

The initial statement to understand is, we are not our thoughts. Inner self-awareness and the use of our intelligence help us understand the mind's proposals. Thus, by observing our thoughts and structuring our life with intelligence, we can begin to free ourselves from the unrestricted control that our mind may have on us. Ultimately, by becoming spiritually grounded, we cultivate spiritual strength that helps us access our intelligence. A spiritually sharpened intelligence is required to control and use our mind more productively.

FOUR

The Secret of Meditation

Human Quality: Tolerance

Swami Bhakti Nipun taught yoga, mantra meditation, oriental philosophy and self-mastery techniques, as well as the science of self-sustenance through traditional organic farming. His latest student, Kaustubha, was an exhausted IT technician. After two redundancies and his sleep ruined due to working multiple nightshifts, Kaustubha realized he needed a stable career path with a holistic life.

Kaustubha had visited the swami's retreat centre in rural Maharashtra for a week for some much-needed rejuvenation. The almost immediate effects of *yoga nidra* and mantra meditation had brought him the sense of well-being he craved. This experience convinced Kaustubha to stay back at the swami's farm to learn more about personal wellness.

Kaustubha was tall, had a broad jaw and brown eyes. His leg shook as if he was always restless and impatient. Although only twenty-five, Kaustubha looked much older due to the dullness of his face. However, Kaustubha would do everything he could not to reveal his chronic fatigue due to broken-down sleep.

Swami Bhakti Nipun on the other hand, was a short guy with an enigmatic smile. Like Kaustubha, the swami did not look his age. His thoughtful countenance, eyes gleaming with confidence and lustrous skin despite being sparsely wrinkled, concealed the truth about his fifty-year-old body. Thanks to years of daily mantra meditation, the swami radiated an effulgent, yet calming power.

The first thing Kaustubha did was sign up for a course on sustainable living at the swami's farm. He wanted to experience what it would be like to live a simple life connected to nature. During the next three months, Kaustubha learnt about soil nutrient cycles, soil water management, tillage, cultivation, seed science and pest and weed management.

After completion of the course, for a hands-on demonstration of his learning, Kaustubha was given a tract of land to develop into a small produce garden over twelve weeks. Hard-working and sincere, Kaustubha and his small team worked very diligently to apply what they had learnt. They chose the right mix of herbs, flowering plants, vegetables and fruit creepers suitable to the soil and the season.

At the end of the twelve weeks, Kaustubha and his team displayed their achievement to Swami Bhakti Nipun. As he arrived, he appreciated an engraved wooden plank hanging at the entrance. The plank read 'Ananda Kaanan—the Forest of Joy'. It was covered with a natural filigree of green vines and creepers. Seeing his spiritual teacher, Kaustubha bowed down and offered a luscious garland of flowers.

'Rajnigandha, the king of fragrant flowers, grown here at Ananda Kaanan!' said an excited Kaustubha. The guru gratefully touched the garland to his forehead in respect.

Folding his hands, the swami showered smiles laden with blessings on his student and his team out of affection.

'Why do you want to turn away from the glamorous world of technology to the simple world of farming, Kaustubha?' asked the guru while tasting some of the various berries and fruits grown and offered to him.

'Swamiji, I've seen it all. The glamour for me is hollow. I am better read and more aware now. And I want to make a positive contribution without destroying our planet. I want to be a peacemaker. We have to shift from the violent industrial agriculture to an agriculture of peace if we want to save the planet. Factory farms are killing poor animals, killing our health, killing our conscience and killing our planet. I can no longer side with destructive forces. I want to live more thoughtfully rather than selfishly,' said an emotional Kaustubha.

'I can see how inspired you are. Let's walk through your garden of joy, shall we?' said the guru.

'Sure swamiji, by the way, it's "the Forest of Joy"', Kaustubha emphasized cheekily.

They both walked through the area. The guru inspected the produce, asked questions and made silent observations.

Upon their return to the starting point, a makeshift hut, the guru spoke, 'I am very impressed with your dedication and I can see how much work you have put into organizing things for my visit. Thank you. You've truly impressed me with your farming skills and your enthusiasm to become a change agent in the world.'

Turning slightly skywards towards a distant tree, the guru spoke further, 'I have noticed that there are no dry or yellow leaves in this entire patch of land. Not even on the plants! You have created this beautiful garden, almost entirely free of any blemishes.'

Excited, Kaustubha replied, 'I am glad you noticed it! I have personally removed all dry foliage down to the last yellow leaf. You won't find any imperfection in Ananda Kaanan.'

Turning back towards Kaustubha, the swami shared a profound insight. 'Kaustubha, the Gita teaches us that life is not all lush and green always. When autumn arrives, life will stand bare naked, without fruits or greens, and eventually the plant of life will grow old and shrivel away. The perfection of life is in learning to accept the yellow leaves of rejection, the dried bloom of the expired flower of success, the unsprouted seeds of fruitless labour and the wilted fruits of missed opportunities. Life is not just about good health, but also treating and tolerating the pests of disease. Life is not all about finding friends, but also being accommodative of those who appear to be weeds,' said the guru, smiling with assertive but compassionate eyes.

Concluding, the swami held Kaustubha by his arms and said, 'My dear son, we must learn to accept change and not spend our energy unproductively avoiding or uprooting it. Howsoever unwilling we may be to part away from our flowering present, we must develop the awareness that it is slowly withering away, and before our season runs out, we must learn to make an offering of our life to the Supreme Lord and our service to His creation.'

mātrā-sparśās tu kaunteya
śītoṣṇa-sukha-duḥkha-dāḥ

āgamāpāyino 'nityās
tāṁs titikṣasva bhārata
(Bhagavad Gita 2.14)

This verse from the second chapter of the Gita shows us a mature way of dealing with the effects of change in life. Both happiness and distress are existential realities and are cyclic in nature like changing seasons. Both are fluctuating and impermanent. Summers are gradually followed by winters. The wise prepare in time and learn to tolerate the inevitable effects of change.

PLACE OF TOLERANCE IN LIFE

'Will my hard work ensure a career which is meaningful and rewarding?'; 'Will the holiday be as enjoyable and comfortable as I expect?'; 'Will my partner understand and respect my feelings when we decide on important matters?'

For all such questions that decide our happiness, Lord Krishna recommends an attitude of tolerance. Tolerance prevents us from attacks of resentment when we are let down. Tolerance helps us mature when we encounter the necessary disappointments in life. It allows us to deliberate on the best approach to adopt in whatever situation we may find ourselves in.

IS DESIRE TO BLAME FOR OUR SUFFERING?

Life's disappointments are mostly based on dissatisfaction. Basing our happiness on enjoyment through the limited faculties of the body and the mind is flawed. This is because our desire for joy is unlimited, but our material agencies are limited.

To deal with such inevitable misery, some philosophers suggest becoming indifferent to desire altogether. They propose the pursuit of desirelessness as the only worthy pursuit. But in doing so, they fail to fully understand the deeper nature of the eternal self. Not just humans, but also birds, animals and insects, who have no self-awareness, are desire-driven beings.

Their very desire for desirelessness goes to show that desire is a permanent, natural and active function of all sentient life forms.

DEALING WITH DISAPPOINTMENTS FROM UNFULFILLED DESIRES

'We are not human beings having a spiritual experience. We are spiritual beings having a human experience,' as a French philosopher has eloquently put it.

The Gita points out the two aspects to our existence; the material aspect as represented by our body-mind unit and the spiritual aspect as represented by the real self, or soul. Without this complete context about the reality of our own existence in the world of matter, we cannot expect to be truly happy or be in a position to properly deal with distress.

THINGS TO CULTIVATE AND AVOID:

1. **Sense:** Recognize your spiritual nature. The real you is an eternal soul resident in your material body and

accompanied by your material mind. Temporary worldly inconveniences become much more bearable when we contemplate the eternality of our spirit.

2. **Nonsense:** Check your mind's tendency to turn to easy escapes from reality—sensual indulgence, drugs, alcohol, staying up all night binge-watching movies, etc. Tolerating our lower urges prevents us from wasting time and also offers us the responsibility to realize our existential relationship with the supreme eternal being, Krishna.

3. **Trans-Sense:** As we begin to appreciate our existential relationship with Krishna, we start seeing difficulties not as pointless problems to tolerate, but as purposeful opportunities provided for our spiritual elevation. This is achieved by actively spiritualizing our existence through transcendental means such as the practice of bhakti-yoga.

FIVE

Quality Determines Success

Human Quality: Gratitude

Dr Lalita Shah was the head of the oncology department at the Government Hospital in Surat. An accomplished author and philanthropist, she also ran Hari Ashraya, a large orphanage in the town. Her orphanage had produced many doctors, engineers, teachers and social workers. Approaching sixty-five years of age, Dr Shah was now looking to retire in Govardhan for the remainder of her life. She was on the lookout for a worthy candidate to replace her as the director of Hari Ashraya. The head of public relations at the orphanage was her first choice.

Jyotsna Shah had an interesting journey at Hari Ashraya. She had been an orphan herself, but with the care of Dr Shah, she blossomed into a smart management graduate from the prestigious Indian Institute of Management, Ahmedabad. She couldn't help but give back to the place that had nurtured her, so she had decided to keep working at the orphanage. Over the years, she had seen the fruits of her work there and felt fulfilled. She would often work beyond her scope, closely working with almost all departments of the organization.

When she had first come to Hari Ashraya, Dr Lalita Shah did not know her full name. Dr Shah had accepted Jyotsna and had given her own surname to this abandoned girl. Today, twenty-two years later, Jyotsna stood tall as a glorious testimony to one noble lady's selfless heart.

With the news of Jyotsna's prospective promotion to the top job spreading, her adversaries had become envious. In particular, Natasha Kapoor, the ambitious head of finance, was furious that she was not in contention. A Shri Rama College gold medallist, Natasha was fiercely competitive and considered second spot to be below her dignity.

A memo was circulated from Dr Shah's office for an upcoming board meeting in two weeks' time. Natasha knew what this meant. Her envy of Jyotsna turned investigative to find something against her self-assigned nemesis. During a friendly lunch in Jyotsna's office, Natasha had noticed that Jyotsna had a fireproof safe in her office closet. Over months, she had noticed that Jyotsna accessed that safe daily before leaving office. 'What could she be storing in that safe? Cash? Donation cheques? Property papers?' Natasha pondered. She then sent a request for a personal appointment with Dr Shah at the earliest to discuss the matter.

'Natasha, while you are the head of finance, I can appreciate your concern for financial transparency at all levels of our organization, but to undertake a surprise audit of the kind you are suggesting is very awkward,' said a concerned Dr Shah.

'Madam, you are planning to retire soon and we need to adopt the best practices. We need to weed out any malpractices before you retire to set gold standards for the future well-being of Hari Ashraya,' replied Natasha.

'All right then, I will accompany you to ensure a smooth execution of your plan. We will start with the management team this evening,' conceded Dr Shah.

It was 4.40 p.m. and there was an unexpected tap on Jyotsna's office door. 'Come in,' she said without looking up while continuing her work. 'Jai Shri Krishna, Jyotsna. How was your day?' asked Dr Shah as she entered along with Natasha, Dr Reddy and Mrs Kulkarni, other members of the senior management.

'Mumma, what are you doing here? You could have called me and I would have come to your office,' said a surprised, confused, but ever respectful Jyotsna. 'Is everything alright?' she asked, looking over Dr Shah's shoulders at her colleagues.

'Let me tell you, Jyo,' Natasha said, stepping forward. 'The management team is making sure that all our organizational resources are secure and accounted for. We all have to disclose assets under our care and for that, Dr Reddy is carrying out a check and Mrs Kulkarni is taking a record. Please don't mind my asking, I am only doing this at the behest of Dr Shah, but do you have any resources that you have not disclosed yet?' asked Natasha.

'No, I don't think so,' said Jyotsna calmly.

'Not even in your secret closet?' blurted out Natasha.

'What do you mean, Nat?' asked Jyotsna, choked.

'I believe you may have something hiding in a locked safe,' poked Natasha.

'Those are my personal belongings . . . Mumma, this is unreal,' said an irritated Jyotsna, turning to Dr Shah.

'Beta, please give them access to that hidden safe you have and let them take a record of things. I know you. This is confidential and organization-wide,' requested Dr Shah.

Jyotsna nodded in agreement and walked to the closet behind her workstation. With jittery hands, she punched the code for the electric safe and opened it for inspection. Dr Reddy checked and there was only a metal box inside. He brought it out, put it on Jyotsna's desk and slowly opened it.

Inside the box was one single item—an old teddy bear with a missing eye.

'I was left outside this orphanage with this toy. This teddy is my only possession from my life before Hari Ashraya,' said Jyotsna with a sad smile. 'I call him Papa and he reminds me daily of my past and of what could have been my future, if it were not for Mumma here,' said a tearful Jyotsna. 'Papa has kept me grounded during my successes and determined during challenges. Papa has fed me gratitude every single day of my life,' concluded Jyotsna as Dr Shah approached her and gave her a big bear hug.

tam sukhārādhyam ṛjubhir, ananya-śaraṇair nṛbhiḥ
kṛtajñaḥ ko na seveta, durārādhyam asādhubhiḥ
(Srimad Bhagavatam 3.19.36)

This wonderful verse from *Srimad Bhagavatam* expresses that the experience of love and joy through devotion is very easy for someone who has the feeling of gratitude in their heart. Let us look around and make a list of things we should be grateful to God or Lord Krishna for.

Our parents, our society and the scores of people who we are connected to. The sun, the moon, the air we breathe, the food we have, our body, mind, intelligence, our abilities, the opportunities in life and the lessons of Karma; these are all gifts of Lord Krishna.

Are we morose because we are not consciously grateful for some of these or are we happy to have taken advantage of these gifts and made our lives better than what it could have been without these? Do we take the opportunity to express our gratitude to Krishna? We should introspect and implement a feeling of gratitude towards God and towards His entire creation.

GRATITUDE CAN BE REVIVED BY:

- Remembering the people who have helped us.
- Remembering the exact details of the nature of how they helped us.
- Contemplating on how their help has affected us and transformed our lives positively.
- Reflecting on how we may have struggled and suffered in the absence of such timely intervention.
- Reciting a silent prayer for their well-being.
- Reciprocating with an appropriate gesture of words or actions at the earliest opportunity.

SIX

Faith in the Supreme Well-Wisher

Human Quality: Faith

Ripudaman Dalbehera, a commander in the king's army, was a quiet giant. His huge physique would silence others despite his infrequent use of speech. He was returning home to his village with his new wife, Nevedita Mahapatra, a gifted sitarist who composed music for the royal orchestra.

While they were crossing the river in a boat, a great storm arose and started to violently shake their boat. An army man, Ripudaman was not fearful of the situation, but Nevedita trembled. As the storm intensified, the situation of the stranded couple in the river looked hopeless. At any moment they would be tossed into the raging waters.

Ripudaman continued sitting quietly—calm and composed, acknowledging the helpless situation, but not getting overwhelmed by it. Nevedita, however, was losing her composure. Out of fear, she screamed at her husband, 'We are going to die! Are you not afraid? This may be the last day of our lives!'

Ripudaman looked at his wife and held her with both his hands to help her calm down.

'We are caught in the eye of the storm and only a miracle can save us now. Death is certain!' an anxious and fearful Nevedita cried out. Ripudaman looked around to take note of a developing whirlwind at a distance. He held Nevedita tighter, pulled her closer and fixed her falling plait of hair behind her ear but remained quiet.

'Why are you acting so indifferently to this calamity? Have you gone deaf? Are you struck dumb out of fear? Tell me what we are going to do. We are going to die! We are going to die!' a hysterical Nevedita yelled louder than the howling winds.

Holding his wife's hand ever so securely, looking around to maintain full awareness of the worsening situation, Ripudaman readied to speak. Then, making his wife sit in front of him on the floor of the boat, Ripu took his sword out of its sheath. This made Nevedita even more puzzled. 'What are you trying to do?' she asked, confused.

Bringing his naked sword close to Nevedita's neck, almost touching it, Ripu asked her reassuringly, 'Are you afraid of my sword at your neck?'

Known for his discreet use of words and their heavy import, Nevedita realized that her husband was serious and was trying to make a point. Collecting herself a little, she responded honestly, 'I am not afraid of this sword as long as you are holding it. I know how much you love me. But I am . . .'

Ripu interjected, 'The same is my answer to this defenceless situation. I know God loves us, and this raging storm is ultimately in His hands.'

Wiping his wife's tears and looking deeply into her eyes, Ripu reassured her, 'I would do whatever is possible to protect you. I will not leave your hand, come what may. But I also realize there is not much either of us can do right now.

'Whatsoever is going to happen, is going to be the will of God. Honey, not a blade of grass moves without God's approval. If we survive, it will be God's grace, and if we don't, I am equally accepting of it as the will of providence,' concluded Ripudaman.

'Now, Nevedita, I want you to calm down first. I need you to be in a mental state to be able to follow my instructions to stay afloat should the boat capsize. We will survive by God's grace, but only if you are able to follow my instructions without drowning in your own fear,' advised Ripudaman.

Hearing her beloved's faithful words, Nevedita felt relieved from the tension drawn by her fears. She realized that allowing her mind to overwhelm her in this terrifying situation was only making things worse and might cost them their lives. Instead, turning her faith towards God, she rescued herself from the tsunami her mind was conjuring and was then ready to face the storm in front of her.

ananyās cintayanto mām
ye janāḥ paryupāsate
teṣāṁ nityābhiyuktānāṁ
yoga-kṣemaṁ vahāmy aham
(Bhagavad Gita 9.22)

This wonderful verse is from the ninth chapter of the Gita. Lord Krishna explains here how by always meditating on Him, we invoke His personal presence in our consciousness and attract His special care in our lives. He is making a promise here, a promise to preserve what we have and to provide what we lack.

By protecting us against our own weaknesses and strengthening our virtues, God personally looks after us when we keep our existential relationship with Him active.

REAL AND APPARENT PROBLEMS

One may argue: does meditating on God remove our problems?

The answer: it definitely can. However, the Gita's philosophical analysis gives us a deeper insight of the problems of the world themselves.

The real nature of the material world: Who can deny that this world is not a place of suffering? It is naive to think of it otherwise in the face of Mondays, the hard struggle for existence, disease, old age and ultimately, death. But all problems related to our material existence are also temporary, in sync with the transient nature of matter itself. All material things have a beginning and an end. Though temporary, all problems do need responsible addressing, but they are temporary.

The real nature of our core being: The Gita points out the core reason for the lack of fulfilment experienced by everyone in this world. While we seek permanent happiness, we only get temporary pleasure (accompanied by lots of inescapable misery). This appetite for permanent happiness is rooted in the permanent nature of the eternal soul.

The real reason for our lack of fulfilment, despite all our freedoms, resources and achievements, is the incompatibility of our spiritual needs with our desire to enjoy matter. This lack of fulfilment is the real problem of our life.

TEMPORARY PROBLEMS AS AN IMPETUS FOR PERMANENT SOLUTIONS

The Gita does not romanticize the temporary nature of the happiness achieved through material means. Nor does it allow irresponsibility or neglect of material problems.

While problems are inescapable, they are not pointless. They are meant to serve as opportunities for us to make deeper spiritual inquiries. Such inquiries find their answer in wisdom texts like the Gita and guide us on how we can revive our innate spiritual nature. Therefore, the problems we face can become an impetus for our spiritual inquiry and ultimately, our spiritual elevation.

GOD'S HELP IN THE MEANWHILE

It is said that a crisis is a terrible thing to miss. Our faith in God gives us strength when none is available on our own account.

Even when God's protection may not immediately remove our problem, at least at the external material level, there is an unfailing benefit of turning towards Him. By connecting with God, we invoke His presence which protects us internally from the fear we possess in our mind.

The mind has an incredible capacity to magnify our problems greater than their actual size, especially when we are faced with issues beyond our resources or capacity to handle. At such times, our mind often traps us in loops of anxiety by obsessively engaging us to think about our problems. The mind also plays horror stories about imagined gloomy possibilities of all that can further go wrong.

Chronic and even clinical depression are the outcomes of such obsessing over problems. Consequently, internally we feel dejected, depleted, disempowered and defeated before we start tackling the problem at hand.

The mental dragon of worrying is tamed and conquered by the weapon of faith in God's omnipotence and omni-benevolence. This divine faith orients us correctly and empowers us to fight the problem and not be held hostage by it.

HOW CAN WE DEAL WITH DISTRESSFUL SITUATIONS IN LIFE?

Accept: Know that distress is an inescapable part of existence in this material world. Accepting the inevitable helps address it better.

Avoid: Be wise and check before you speak, plan or do. Don't invite more trouble.

Adjust: Adapt to an unavoidable and unfixable situation. Better to bend than to break. Life need not be just a 'win-lose' competition. Don't compromise your intelligence, but compromise using your intelligence.

Amend: Relook at the problem from different perspectives. It might not be as bad as the mind perceives it to be. Re-script your inner narrative and approach the problem again.

Transcend: Use spiritual wisdom to elevate your consciousness to a transcendental platform beyond the range of material happiness and distress. We are neither that body nor those thoughts; we are a divine spark of consciousness and the Supreme Lord is our witness, shelter and dear friend. Attuning to our spiritual identity empowers us beyond our material limitations and grants us spiritual bliss despite circumstantial ups and downs.

The ultimate solution to the cyclic loop of happiness and distress is in reinstating ourselves in our true spiritual identity. Real freedom from both temporary and permanent problems lies in reviving our loving relationship with our divine source, Krishna.

SEVEN

The Tree and the Carpenter Team

Human Quality: Maturity

Jagdeep Singh Gurjar, born in Haryana but raised in Punjab, was a devout turban-clad handsome man. Well-built, qualified and an experienced carpenter, Jagdeep took pride in his work and craftsmanship. He was hired by Mr Singhania, a cloth merchant, to build the interiors of his new shop. Mr Singhania got Jagdeep's reference from a business friend who endorsed the quality of Jagdeep's work and his temperament.

One day, as soon as Jagdeep reached the worksite, he found a nail sticking out of the back tyre of his workshop van. Not sure about the scale of the damage, Jagdeep pushed the vehicle slowly to the side. Clearly it wasn't his day when while undocking his tool bag, the power drill fell down on his foot. A little hurt and now the owner of a damaged tool, Jagdeep looked pensively at the sky.

After taking a small break to gather himself, Jagdeep returned to the worksite while Mr Singhania waited for him. 'Jaggi, look, if you want, you can take the day off. I understand your situation,' offered Mr Singhania.

'Paaji, they say if you have a hammer, it's time to work. We're set for action,' Jagdeep spoke in jest. Impressed by his commitment and character, Mr Singhania fetched some fresh sugarcane juice to help them cool off the heat.

After the day's work, Mr Singhania helped Jagdeep tow away the broken-down van to a mechanic's garage. Mr Singhania then dropped Jagdeep to his residence. But before he drove off, he saw Jagdeep do something interesting before entering his house.

As soon as he got out of Mr Singhania's car, Jagdeep went straight to a tree opposite his house. Holding a branch in his two hands, it looked like he was making a prayer. Looking intently from a distance, Mr Singhania saw how, upon entering his house, Jagdeep cheerfully lifted everyone's spirits. He first bowed to touch his mother's feet, tickled and lifted his son on his shoulders and held his wife and daughter's hands lovingly.

The next day, when Jagdeep reached the worksite, Mr Singhania asked him, 'Jaggi, if you don't mind, can I ask you something?'

'Of course, Paaji,' replied Jagdeep.

'Yesterday was a terrible day for you with nothing going your way. But after I dropped you, I saw that you went to that tree first and then brightened everybody's face with happiness at your home. What's your secret for such optimism?' asked an inquisitive Mr Singhania.

'O Paaji, that tree is my friend, Tamarind Singh. No matter what happens in my day, before I enter home, I go to Tamarind Singh first and deposit all my sour experiences with him,' Jagdeep replied.

Amused, Mr Singhania smiled.

Unzipping his toolkit, Jaggi concluded, 'Paaji, it's a win-win equation. My family does not deserve the sourness of my day's negative experiences and that Tamarind Singh has a taste for sour things anyway!'

'That's wonderful,' said Mr Singhania. 'But do things not pile up eventually? Do you not feel emotionally pent-up by dealing with your real problems in this abstract way?'

Placing his tools on his workstation, Jaggi replied, 'Paaji, you are right. Tamarind Singh serves well in that passive capacity for clearing my immediate negativity. But, from time to time, I need someone to respond to my problems, someone to empathize with me and encourage me.'

'And I would imagine that would be your wife or close friend?' added Mr Singhania.

'Paaji, luckily my lovely wife is my closest friend and my greatest supporter. We share a very close bond. But for both of us, our go-to person for serious matters is someone else,' replied Jaggi.

'Who? Your mother? I hope you don't mind my asking all this. I've never met anyone like you and so I'm curious,' said Mr Singhania sheepishly.

'Not a problem Paaji, I appreciate your honesty. And no, it is not my mother either. For dealing with the real problems of my life, I turn to God,' said Jaggi with a calm smile.

'God! And how do you communicate with God?' asked Mr Singhania with a slight tinge of doubt in his eyes.

'Through prayer, Paaji. When I pray sincerely and open my heart to God with utmost honesty, I receive the insight

and strength to deal with the impending problem at hand,'
said Jaggi in a matter of fact way.

'Are you serious? So, you are telling me that to deal with
real problems in life, you pray and everything falls into place
mystically?' asked Mr Singhania with a changed pitch in his
voice.

'No Paaji. I'm afraid I don't think you understand how
praying works. Firstly, praying is never a replacement for our
acting responsibly to address our issues. Praying is not a magic
wand to solve all problems.

'When Arjuna prayed to Krishna in the Gita, he did
not imagine that on account of his praying, everything
would be resolved and he need not do anything for his
protection in the war. In his prayers to Krishna's gigantic
universal form, Arjuna beseeches the omnipotent Lord but
does not excuse himself from his worldly duties. Prayer is
not a call for retirement from our responsibilities, but a
call for reinforcement towards them. After praying, Arjuna
fought diligently, freed from all self-doubt and confusion,'
explained Jaggi.

'So, you're saying that praying is not a substitute for our
dealing with problems. What is the practical contribution of
praying then?' asked Mr Singhania.

'Paaji, with anything that we face in this world, there are
things that are beyond our control. Our mind worries about
these problem areas, gets restless and feels helpless against
them. Our praying to God is a reminder to ourselves that
things that are out of our hands are not entirely out of control.
What is unmanageable for us will be managed by someone far
greater than us.'

'I see. I guess that's why people experience peace of mind through praying,' added Mr Singhania.

'Exactly. Now Paaji, once our mind is calm and collected, having entrusted that which is beyond our control in the safe and capable hands of God, we are in a far better shape to deal with that which is within the scope of our control. Acting out our part diligently is an expression of the sincerity of our prayer to God. When we act responsibly, with faith and without lethargy, we attract God's special grace to better utilize our abilities and resources to deal with the problem.'

'Oh, I see your connection between peace of mind and focusing the mind better,' said Mr Singhania, nodding thoughtfully.

'And ultimately, Paaji, when we pray, we experience a spiritual connection with the Supreme Lord and that grants us not just peace, focus and strength, but also the realization of our own spiritual nature. Self-realization is the real solution to all our existential problems. Praying enables us to optimize our worldly existence and transcend its grip on us altogether,' concluded Jaggi.

'Well, thank you so much, Jaggi. I live on the seventh floor of a high-rise building and do not have a tamarind tree in front of my apartment, but I will certainly add thoughtful prayer to my life now,' said Mr Singhania appreciatively.

It is said:

piteva putraṁ karuṇo nodvejayati yo janam
viśuddhasya hṛṣīkeśas-tūrṇaṁ tasya prasīdati

Just as a father is affectionate to his children and never becomes the cause of their fear or anxieties, Lord Krishna is very quickly pleased with those pure-minded souls who are compassionate to all creatures, and avoid becoming the source of pain, harassment, fear or anxiety for others. (*Bhakti-rasāmāta-sindhu*, *Pūrva-vibhāga* 2.117)

NEED FOR EMOTIONAL MATURITY

Emotional maturity includes the ability to deal with life's realities in constructive and productive ways. Faced with challenging situations, we often grow irritable and are impelled to thoughtless actions. This happens under the spell of frustration or anger. In such a state, we react in regrettable ways, unnecessarily using harsh words or other forms of passive, active or micro aggression. We thereby become generators of avoidable conflict and pain. Most of the time, our victims are the people closest to us.

It is often found that behind our impulsive reactions is a sense of grief or some hidden insecurity. Our losses cause us grief and our insecurities cause us inner instability. Consequently, we either fight or flee. Thus, unable to deal with life's challenges in a mature way, we either attack in resentment or try to escape out of fear.

CULTIVATING MATURITY IN LIFE

Maturity in relationships and decision-making is a combination of three things.

- **Sukriti:** acting with nobility, free from gross exploitative tendencies.
- **Kripa:** God's grace drawn in our hearts through our selfless service for others.

- **Vivek:** Wise discrimination born out of experience and learning.

Maturity is the balance between courage and consideration. When we express our feelings and convictions with courage, balanced with consideration for the feelings and convictions of others, we have matured.

EIGHT

Krishna as the Centre of Our Life

Human Quality: Devotion

It was the day of Holi, the festival of colours in Vrindavan. All the cowherds assembled in front of Mother Yashoda's palace and they started calling out to their best friend, Krishna.

'Kanhaiya come out, we promise we don't have water guns in our hands . . .' the boys yelled out, giggling.

Inside Nandabhavan, Krishna hid in Nand Baba's room and called for Mother Yashoda. 'Maiya, please go and tell my friends that I am not home today.'

'Why, lalla?' Mother asked.

Krishna explained, 'I have played so many pranks on my friends all year around. Now they have all come well prepared to pay me back with water guns and coloured powder prepared from the roots of turmeric, beetroot and other coloured gifts of nature. I'm sure they will attack me from all sides. They have all united against Me and it is going to be a one-sided affair!'

'But Kanha, these beautiful colours fill everyone's heart with joy. Do you know what these Holi colours represent?'

'No, Maiya,' said Krishna with a thoughtful expression on His face.

'My dear lalla, red represents love. Yellow is the colour of learning. Green represents growth and pink is a boon of care. Similarly, purple is a blessing of excellence, blue a call for valour and orange a symbol of freedom. When friends throw these different colours on each other, they are wishing these great blessings on you. Who won't want the happiness represented by these colours in their life?' Mother Yashoda asked as she caressed Krishna's head.

Krishna, however, protested about the one-sided contest and requested Mother Yashoda to comply with His command of love.

Yielding to her charming son, Mother Yashoda came out of the palace and spoke loudly, 'All of you lovely boys, please know that Krishna's not home.'

'He has personally told me this just now . . .' added Mother Yashoda in a whisper and with a naughty smile.

Understanding the matter, Madhumangal, one of the leaders of the group, said loudly, 'I cannot believe you. I think Krishna is readying Himself for a colour battle.'

Mother Yashoda loudly said, 'Okay Madhu, only because you don't believe me and are insisting on an inspection, you come inside and see for yourself that Krishna is not here.'

Madhumangal winked at the boys and entered Nandabhavan. Directed silently by Mother Yashoda, after making animated sounds of looking for Krishna in other rooms, Madhu stood in the veranda and loudly spoke, 'I think Mother Yashoda is telling the truth. That butter thief is probably locked and arrested in some old Gopi's house. Let me call all the boys in for some refreshments before we leave.'

Immediately, Krishna came running out of Nand Baba's room, put His hand on Madhu's mouth and took him inside.

'Madhu, you are my dear friend and you need to help Me. I am afraid the boys are going to pounce on Me with colour from all directions. Go tell them that I am not home and take them away,' said Krishna with a child's fear.

Madhu replied, 'Oh, Krishna, as You already know, I'm a VERY truthful person. I won't be telling any lies.'

Knowing Madhu's weakness, Krishna took a plate of sweets from under His bed and offered a bribe. 'Then I guess I will feed these nice laddoos and rabri to the monkeys.'

Immediately taking the plate from Krishna's hands, Madhumangal said, 'Well, I guess what is between friends should remain between friends.'

Madhu ate, promised and left.

Outside, Madhumangal, his hands held high for everyone to see his fingers crossed, spoke softly, 'Boys, as loyal as I am to Krishna, I must share my findings with you in all honesty. When I say that Krishna is not at home, He did not bribe me with sweets and He won't enjoy a piggy ride on our backs after a colour contest, how many of you will believe me?'

Pausing for a moment, Madhu answered his own question loudly, 'All of you believe me . . .'

Understanding Madhu's intention, the boys roared in unison, 'Yes we believe you, entirely!'

'So, let's leave and go enjoy the colour battle elsewhere,' responded Madhu aloud.

With loud footsteps, the boys walked away from Nandabhavan. Then, turning around again, they ran at full pace into the house and then to the room where Krishna was hiding.

Caught unprepared and unsuspecting, Krishna had nowhere to run. Each boy personally put colour on Krishna's cheeks and forehead.

Immediately, Mother Yashoda and Mother Rohini brought Krishna's water gun and bags of coloured powder. Smiling, Krishna whistled to Balaram to get into action and everyone laughed in joy. And in this way, the festival of colours took place right in the veranda of King Nanda Maharaj's palace.

The *Srimad Bhagavatam* 10.14.36 describes

> *tāvad rāgādayaḥ stenās*
> *tāvat kārā-gṛhaṁ gṛham*
> *tāvan moho 'ṅghri-nigaḍo*
> *yāvat kṛṣṇa na te janāḥ*

Vrindavan is a place where Krishna is the centre of everyone's life. When God or Krishna is not the centre of our lives, then our homes, our desires and our ambitions, all become shackles and fill our life with anxiety and dissatisfaction. Why? Anxiety, from the *fear born of disconnection* with our ultimate shelter, the Supreme Personality of Godhead. And dissatisfaction, due to the absence of *the intrinsic purpose of existence* which is the pursuit of loving union of the creation with its creator.

Friends, our anxiety and dissatisfaction beseech us to inquire without prejudice their root cause. The downward spiral of individual, social, ecological and global degradation is only a proof of unsatisfactory responses to these existential inquiries and unfulfilled needs of the soul.

When faith in God is covered, atheism prevails in six forms:

1. **Default Atheists:** Those who disbelieve even though they have never really thought or inquired deeply about the subject of God. They are happy-go-lucky, often born of or associated with other default atheists.

2. **Reductionist Atheists:** Often those who proclaim 'seeing is believing'. They try to superimpose the valid partial truths of their limited material experience to explore and verify an equally valid but non-material dimension. Their major fault lies in equating one fragment of reality that they can observe and experiment, with the totality of reality that lies beyond both the limited power of their investigative tools and the limited ability of their own comprehension. Their approach is often backward engineering, employed to establish their premeditated hypothesis of the non-existence of God.

3. **Philosophical Atheists:** Those who arrogantly profess that belief in God is intellectually immature and philosophically naive. Often, their arguments are ill-founded, being tainted with biases, dishonest lines of reasoning or inconclusive speculations presented as axiomatic truths. They fight religion, often driven by subjective standards of morality. They often take literalistic stands without attempting to understand the essence of religious precepts.

4. **Emotional Atheists:** Those whose disbelief comes from the decadence of modern-day religion, inconsiderate and

harmful behaviour of religious fanatics or as a loss of faith caused by unfortunate problems in their own lives.

5. **Covered Atheists:** Those who pose as theists but assert through their own speculative means that we are all ultimately God, only temporarily deluded.

6. **Psychological Atheists:** Those who profess belief in God but repeatedly demonstrate their inability to practically live a Godly life due to attachment to worldliness. Their claim of belief in God falls short when they act in unethical ways without regard for expected standards of genuine Godly life.

MISCONCEPTIONS AND ATHEISM

Do not be fooled; all these categories of people have always existed. Atheism is not a new development on account of scientific or technological advancement. But the desacralization of the world through modern science is a recent innovation. Science and religion were never positioned against each other. They rather complement each other. French biologist Louis Pasteur put it well: 'A little science takes you away from God, but more of it takes you to Him.'

Some people lose their faith because they approach God with a poor conception of God in mind. When reduced as a fulfiller of our desires, as a problem-solver or as a protector of our assets, God is seen as a means to our worldly motivations. When material desires are unfulfilled or in the face of problems in life, when all these temporary expectations are not met, loss of faith occurs.

Others argue about the non-existence of a merciful God in the presence of evil in the world. 'If there were a kind-hearted God, how could he allow little children to be shot dead by a psychopath?' they argue. Without learning and understanding what God allows us to do and what He expects us to do, they shift the blame on God when it actually lies on the members of an ungodly society.

PURPOSE OF MATERIALITY AND PROFITS OF SPIRITUALITY

The Gita explains that unless we see the material world's design in the light of its purpose, all our happiness and suffering, and our progress or lack thereof, remains pointless. Gita wisdom explains that the point of this world is to point beyond it, to the spiritual reality.

By understanding our own spiritual nature, underlying our material body, we can come to realize that we exist in this world not to simply consume, defend and die. Everyone seeks permanent happiness, eternal existence and complete knowledge. Why? Because these are the attributes of our core spiritual identity. Our material endeavours can only satisfy these spiritual needs unsatisfactorily.

Gita wisdom explains that by raising our consciousness spiritually, established in our indestructible spiritual identity, we taste real freedom and get rid of all our fears. It is our common spiritual essence that unites us all. Such spiritual commonality brings about real equality in society, away from sexism, casteism, racism and sectarianism. With such spiritual education, we come to see the world as a means to

God and become thoughtful to respect nature and denounce our exploitative tendencies.

Religious life devoid of genuine spiritual cultivation and a non-religious life without honest inquiry about the very purpose of life are counterproductive.

The gratification of the body only gives temporary satisfaction and generates frustration, be one religious or non-religious. It is in the fulfilment of the soul where lies lasting peace and happiness. And this spiritual fulfilment takes care of our feverish worldly ailments—individual and collective.

NINE

The Mystery of Blessings

Human Quality: Blessings

There was a king who would ride out of his palace every day in his royal chariot to attend meetings with public administrators. Two beggars, Raju and Madhu, would wait for him outside the town hall. At the king's arrival, Raju would say out loud, 'Blessed is he, who is helped by the king.' Madhu too would look at the king and pronounce, 'Blessed is he, who is helped by the Supreme Lord.' Flattered to hear Raju's praises of him and taking Madhu to be a sentimentalist with no knack for worldly practicality, the king would pass by with a royal flutter.

Appeased by Raju, and to teach worldly dealings to Madhu, the king once decided to reciprocate with Raju. He directed his royal chefs to make a big cake of Mysore Pak and gave them a gold ring to hide in the middle. The next day, as the two beggars resounded their statements of glorification, the king called Raju close to him and as Madhu watched, the king clapped for his servants to bring and gift the Mysore Pak to Raju. While repeating his glorification, 'Blessed is he, who is helped by the king', Raju walked away. The king looked at Madhu who folded his hands in respect of the king and repeated his glorification, 'Blessed is he, who is helped by the Supreme Lord.' Dismissing his presence, the king walked away.

Meanwhile, looking at the sweetmeat, Raju condemned the king, 'His Royal Miserliness has gifted me this stupid slab of sugar! How much of it can I eat before it goes foul? Better I sell it and get some money.' Thinking like this, Raju took the sweet to Madhu and asked if he would like to buy it off him. Madhu thought of buying it to offer it to the temple deity of Srinathji who was known to be fond of sweets.

'Such a big cake of Mysore Pak! It was made in the royal kitchen, so only the very best ingredients must have been used. Truly, Srinathji will love it.'

Madhu gave all the money he had saved from begging over the past few weeks and purchased the cake to offer to the Lord.

Then he went to the temple and handed over the sweet to the priest. The pujari made the offering to the deity and afterwards asked Madhu what he'd like to do with it. Madhu requested that the cake be cut into pieces and distributed to temple visitors as he waited.

With every piece of the now sanctified Mysore Pak being distributed, Madhu's joy knew no bounds. The distribution of the Lord's prasad brought great satisfaction to his heart. At the end, the priest offered one last sizeable piece to the impoverished beggar.

'Madhu, did you eat anything today? Here, take this big piece as a gift of blessings from Srinathji,' said the priest, offering the last remaining piece along with some tulsi leaves and a flower garland from the deity.

Madhu took the piece to his hut in great ecstasy and honoured the sacred sweet with devotion. Soon he found an object appearing in his mouth as the final bits of the sweet melted away. He took this unknown article out and was amazed to see that it was a gold ring studded with jewels.

'O Srinathji, what have You done with me!' exclaimed Madhu with eyes smiling in disbelief.

The next day, the king came out again with his royal entourage. He noticed that only the first beggar was present there. The king looked at him and said, 'You are still begging? What happened to the cake I gave you yesterday?'

Raju explained, 'Your royal highness, I am not so fond of sweets. I sold that cake to my other beggar friend, Madhu. By your grace, I bought enough rice from the money to feed me for a month. Thank you. Blessed is he, who is helped by the king.'

Hearing this, the king laughed and loudly exclaimed, 'No! Blessed is he, who is helped by the Lord.'

And so friends it is described,

athāpi te deva padāmbuja-dvaya-
prasāda-leśānugṛhīta eva hi
jānāti tattvaṁ bhagavan-mahimno
na cānya eko 'pi ciraṁ vicinvan

This is a prayer by Brahma to Lord Krishna. He says: My Lord, if one is blessed by even a slight trace of the mercy of Your lotus feet, one can easily come to realize the extraordinary greatness of Your personality. Without Your favour, however, those who speculate to understand the Supreme Personality of Godhead, continue to exert themselves fruitlessly. Even the learned oracles on scriptures are incapable of knowing You on their own strength. Their intellectual gymnastics are only so much labour for sweat. (*Srimad Bhagavatam* 10.14.29)

WHAT ARE BLESSINGS?

Life in all its simplicity and detail is saturated with blessings. The air we breathe, the space we occupy, the food we grow for our subsistence and the opportunities that life makes possible for us are favours that we have done nothing special to deserve. Aren't these gifts of existence all blessings in our life?

When we utilize what we have and work to please the Supreme Lord, the spiritually advanced and our wise elders, the pleasure of those whom we seek to please is a special blessing we attract.

At a spiritual level, it is actually God or Krishna who is manifesting His blessing through a great soul who is pleased by us. Such souls have pure intentions, integrity of character and maturity in their devotion to God. Through these divine virtues, they are strongly connected to the Lord and act as conduits of His grace. If a devotee of the Lord is pleased by our words, thoughts or deeds and blesses us, then through that devotee's prayerful good wishes, God's special grace reaches us.

HOW CAN WE INVOKE THE TRANSFORMATIVE BLESSINGS OF EXALTED PEOPLE?

Blessings are received when we do the following: *Submissively hear* the instructions of our elders, mentors and scriptures, sincerely *serve* those instructions and successfully *please* God and our worthy seniors.

WHAT ARE THE EFFECTS OF BLESSINGS BY A WORTHY PERSON?

We achieve fulfilment of our positive desires and destruction of the obstacles on our path of spiritual advancement.

Without comparing our blessings with the blessings others have received, we can be thankful by appreciating all that we have. Then we can see how fortunate we are and can find inspiration to move forward in life with vigour to win over even tough challenges. Blessings thus grant us an inspired heart with renewed strength and free of obstructions.

HOW CAN WE UTILIZE OUR BLESSINGS?

Blessings act out through a grateful heart. At any stage or phase of life, we can either count our misfortunes or count our blessings. Whichever list we read more often will mould our temperaments. Appreciating the vast and complex world around us, so minutely fine-tuned for our use, our heart should naturally grow warmer in gratitude.

Gratitude has two aspects—the *experience of gratitude* and the *expression of gratitude*.

When we value what we have and take note of what we have received, we can *count our blessings* with a grateful heart.

And when we put that gratitude into action, expressing our indebtedness by using our gifts for the betterment of others, then we *make our blessings count*.

The Gita explains that all of us are spirit souls with an unalienable relationship with God or Krishna. With the cultivation of our dormant spirituality, our invisible bond with the Lord becomes factually manifest. At that stage, we too become conduits of His grace. We become decorated with virtues like thoughtful execution of our duties, compassion and respect for all, willingness to serve others without expectations, freedom from envy and loving devotion to God and His creation.

Let us not just be content with collecting blessings to benefit our life, but also commit to making our blessings count. Let us also work on elevating our consciousness to become a source of blessings for others around us.

TEN

Team Spirit

Human Quality: Association

Abhijith Pillai was a fresh graduate in power engineering. His promising college placement came on account of his good grades, amiable personality and confident communication skills. After having visited his hometown of Trichy in Tamil Nadu and taking the blessings of his parents, Abhijith returned to his college in Visakhapatnam. The farewell ceremony at the college was memorable and the lift-off into the future was booked for the coming weekend.

To work on his first power plant project, Abhijith had to move from Visakhapatnam to Jamshedpur. His newly bought second-hand car was packed with all his clothes, plenty of food and a bunch of farewell cards. This was the first time Abhijith was travelling long distance by road.

Abhijith's father, Srinrsimha Rao, a retired government officer, had offered to accompany him, but Abhi had thoughtfully declined the offer considering his dad's health. A robust 'road trip packing list' was then prepared by Mr Rao. Abhijith was commissioned to stick the checklist to the inside of the car's windshield, tick each item at the earliest and send a picture of the same on WhatsApp the day before beginning.

With 800 kilometres ahead of him, Abhijith's lone road trip through the countryside, and for a promising future, was no less romantic than any Bollywood love story. The scheduled eighteen hours were planned to be covered with several pit stops accompanied throughout by his favourite songs, and his questionable singing along with them.

Too busy changing the track to play the next on the car's sound system, Abhijith's inattention got him stuck in a thick patch of muddy countryside. Dad's checklist item 'stick to the playlist' was overlooked, and now the novice traveller was paying the penalty. A frenzied change of gears and furious hits on the accelerator didn't seem to matter. Mother Nature reduced the fast and furious to the feeble and fruitless. The beautiful Purunakatak skies were looking down to host an unscheduled guest for the night. 'Bug spray', another item on Dad's checklist, was suddenly making sense to Abhijith.

Wandering alone for help on the country road, Abhi was spotted by a lone farmer who called out to him. Turning around, Abhijith rushed to the man on the bullock cart with unsure anticipation. But before Abhi could say anything, Badrinath, the farmer, addressing his bull, said, 'Chandru, this babu needs our help, his motorcar is glued to the mud.'

Abhijith understood that this was not the first time this judicious farmer was helping out a stranger.

'Quick babu, Chandru's wife doesn't like it when he gets home late,' said the farmer as he made place for Abhijith to sit next to him on the cart.

Within a short while, the three accidental friends reached the site of the stranded car. Placing the bullock cart in front and tying a thick coir rope from the middle of his cart's yoke to the tow hook on the car's bumper, Badrinath started directing the pull.

'Chandru, Bhima, Angad, Nandi, come on boys, show us some veggie power.'

'Chandru, look, Bhima is doing most of the work, come on son!'

'Move it Nandi, get out of Chandru's way!'

'Well done Angad, now give Chandru a helping push.'

As the quick-witted countryman shouted these impassioned encouragements, Abhijith felt confused; he could see only one bull. Who were these other names?

'Boys, we are almost there, one last push together!' Badri yelled.

To Abhi's great relief, the car was finally pulled out of the muddy muck.

With the car set free, Abhijith offered some money to Badri, who declined.

'The boys don't like to be tipped for their goodwill, sahib.'

Still unsure of what he had witnessed, Abhijith said to Badri, 'I'm so grateful for your help and to Chandru, your bull. But what were the other names you were calling out? I see only one bull here.'

Badrinath explained, 'Babu, our Chandru has grown old and he also went blind in one eye last year. Mind you, he's still very strong and thoroughly enjoys a good workout. Life taught me that overconfidence in our own inadequacies hinders us more than the incidental lack of our resources. Therefore,

I never allow self-doubt to disempower me. I make sure that my boy is thinking that he's part of a great team. By calling out these names, Chandru thinks that he's not alone and can depend on his mates.'

The *Bhagavatam* 1.10.11 describes,

sat-saṅgān mukta-duḥsaṅgo, hātuṁ notsahate budhaḥ
kīrtyamānaṁ yaśo yasya, sakṛd ākarṇya rocanam

When we associate with like-minded, positive people, we can win over the darkest influences of negativity in our lives. Individually overcoming our weaknesses is often an uphill task, especially when we are disappointed with ourselves or with the direction of our life. But the sooner we beg, borrow or steal the association of those who are actively working towards freedom from lethargy, dread born of self-pity and who are acquainted with a higher vision of life's purpose, the quicker things start to turn around positively for us.

A LOT IS NOT ACHIEVED ALONE

The Gita explains that the existence of the eternal soul in the realm of temporary matter is riddled with problems. The recommendation is to associate with the wise and make a collective effort for individual perfection. We all are ultimately social beings and thus, we gain strength in the association of others. Therefore, a healthy team spirit needs to be cultivated, nurtured and blossomed for our ongoing inspiration and enthusiasm in life.

The three steps in improving team spirit are:

Step 1: Connect with a Greater Purpose

Help people in your team find greater meaning in their daily chores by conveying and communicating the purpose of your efforts clearly. Individually, be clear about your reasons for pursuing a goal and take responsibility for your role in the team. Without individual responsibility, even the best plans fail. And without collective strength, the barriers of old habits are often too strong to break.

Step 2: Be Engaged Emotionally

When we are emotionally connected to a purpose, our subconscious mind pushes us to achieve our objectives with greater vigour and zest. The success of any plan is based on how deeply we engage with its execution.

Step 3: Create a Culture of Collaboration

In a *cooperative* culture, support is provided only when asked for. In a *collaborative* culture, assistance is offered proactively by the members of the team to each other. A collaborative culture is built by helping the team envision a higher common goal. Success is better approached when many work together to achieve a single goal desired by each one.

ELEVEN

The Conqueror Conquered

Human Quality: Spirituality

'King of kings, the lord of the world, Alexander the Great has called for you. Comply and come with me,' the soldier ordered the lone mendicant who lived by the shore of the Ganga.

The tall and lean sadhu sitting cross-legged in meditation slowly opened his eyes and spoke, 'King of kings? Lord of the world? I think you are mistaken, either about the person you have described and named or about the person you have been sent to call. I have no interest in meeting any kings.'

'Audacious! How could you refuse the orders of the lord of life?' the soldier shouted, not expecting such a response.

'You sound very loyal. It is a noble quality. Now do me a favour, tell me why do you call this person the lord of life?' requested the monk.

'My lord can take life and he can spare life . . . at the will of his sword!' replied the impassioned soldier.

'I see . . . but has he been able to give life and revive any of his dead soldiers?' the sage asked thoughtfully.

'How dare you!' yelled the soldier in rebuke.

Getting off his horse in a fit of rage, the young soldier tied the unprotesting sage and brought the captive to Alexander's camp.

This was the first of the sages Alexander was to meet in India and each of these meetings, as folklore has it, was overflowing with pristine wisdom.

'Attention! Attention! The Lord of the World! The Shining Lamp of Glory! The Jewel of the Argead Dynasty! Alexander the Great is arriving . . . All rise!' announced a camp guard.

Upon entering and seeing the calm captive in a corner, Alexander spoke in a protesting voice, 'This is no way to treat a poor guest, Cleitus the Black,' said Alexander, while asking General Cleitus to release the sage.

'I apologize for the lack of courtesy shown to you, dear sir,' offered Alexander to the sage.

'Actually, I wish to learn a few things about India's sages. Tell me first, what is that clay mark on your forehead?' requested the king.

Pointing to the *gopi-chandan tilak* on his forehead, the sage said, 'This "clay mark" is called a tilak and it is an insignia of freedom and fearlessness.'

'Fearlessness! My favourite word. Explain further,' said the king in a commanding tone.

'The two parallel vertical lines of the tilak represent the two lotus feet of the Supreme Lord and the small mark underneath them represents tulsi, a sacred leaf that always adorns His feet. A devotee who wears this tilak takes shelter in the Supreme Father. He sees everyone equally and the entire world as his home. Thus, being among his own brethren everywhere and always under the Lord's protection, a devotee is always free and fearless.'

'A sign of universal brotherhood . . . interesting. Tell me a little about yourself now,' requested Alexander further.

'O warrior, I am neither a destitute nor a king; neither Indian nor Greek; neither a man nor a woman; neither homeless nor settled; neither black nor white; neither tall nor short; neither fat nor thin; neither ugly nor beautiful; neither this body nor my mind. I am an eternal, transcendental, spiritual soul and consciousness is my symptom. I was in the past, am in the present and will continue to be in all the future to come. I am a child of the Supreme Personality of Godhead, and so are you,' said the serene sage with a gentle smile.

'That was quite an introduction,' said an amused Alexander.

'I also know something very specific about you that even you don't know yourself,' pointed out the monk.

'Surprise me,' said the king.

'I can tell you, but be prepared. It would be scary to admit, especially in front of your generals and soldiers,' said the sage.

'Scary? I am Alexander the Great!' retorted the king.

The sage said, 'Very well then, to tell you honestly, you are actually a servant of my servants.'

Pouncing from his chair and drawing his sword out, the king shrieked, 'What did you call me?'

Unfazed by a dozen swords drawn at him, the sage remarked, 'I told you, the truth I know about you is going to shake your world and scare you. Are you strong enough to hear how?'

Putting his sword on the sage's neck, Alexander said, 'Yes, tell me and it better be good!'

'O king, I am a devout servant of the Lord and by the strength of my loving devotion, I have captured Him in my heart. By His strength I have won over the six inner enemies—lust, anger, greed, attachment, pride and envy. These great commanders-in-chief no longer rule me. Rather, they are subservient to my control.

'On the other hand, although you have defeated many enemies on the outside, you are quite clearly under the grip of these undisputed inner overlords of human society. Just see, right now you are helplessly acting under the command of anger. You are commanded by that which I have complete command over. And thus, you are a servant of my servants. Is that not so?' asked the sage instructively.

With his head bowed in admission, Alexander asked for the sage to be released with honour.

Friends, Krishna says in the Gita 4.38,

na hi jñānena sadṛśaṁ, pavitram iha vidyate
tat svayaṁ yoga-saṁsiddhaḥ, kālenātmani vindati

There is nothing more empowering than transcendental spiritual knowledge. It is the purest knowledge available to mankind. Why is it the purest? Because it removes all self-ambiguity, confusion and aimlessness in life and positions us on the real platform of inner freedom.

As soon as one becomes acquainted with the science of the self, one is able to clearly see one's core nature, needs and connection with the world around. This spiritual avenue raises us beyond the attacks of insults thrown at the body or disappointments faced by the mind.

But in the absence of self-knowledge, we are misled, either by our own sensual cravings or by material propagandists who are expert at provoking our material identities for their gain. With real spiritual knowledge, one is able to have a drone view of material reality with all its sensual enticements and mental traps.

WHAT DO WE STAND TO GAIN BY SUCH TRANSCENDENTAL KNOWLEDGE?

When one connects with the spiritual knowledge of the soul, one's eternal connection with the Supreme gets activated. Harnessing non-material, spiritual inspiration, stemming from the core of our spiritual being, then becomes available to us.

Recognizing our core identity as a non-material spirit soul who is endowed with the tool of the mind to operate the machine of the body liberates us in a practical way. It grants us a third person view of our own mind-body system. This sense of distance from our own physical and psychological identities grants us the greater autonomy required for better self-governance at both the physical and mental levels.

Short-term gain: Better mind control for greater determination to change our bad habits, increased concentration, the capacity to win over challenges and freedom from disturbing thoughts.

Long-term gain: Self-actualization through spiritual self-realization. This grants us access to deep inner fulfilment through a purpose-driven meaningful life. Lasting inner peace and joy is available in connection with the Lord.

Friends, we must dedicate some time to cultivate spiritual knowledge of the soul if we are at all serious about initiating a positive revolution in our lives for the collective good of the world.

TWELVE

The Mystery of the Chessboard

Human Quality: Self-Improvement

The Gupta Empire of ancient India is often credited for bringing to the world the game called chess today.

In its original form, chess was called *chaturänga*, or 'four limbed' (chaturänga = chatura [four] + anga [limbed]). The four limbs referred to the four sides of the playing board called the *ashtäpada*, an 8x8 square board with its four divisions of the military: infantry, cavalry, elephantry and chariotry as represented by their modern makeover in the pawn, the knight, the bishop and the rook, respectively.

From India, chaturänga was introduced to Persia and the name transformed into *chatrang*, which would evolve into *shatranj* since the Arabs lacked the native phonetics 'ch' and 'ng'. From there, the game spread to other parts of the world.

So, the man who had conceived of the game of chess went to the king and presented his gaming innovation in the royal court. The game conquered the imagination of the king, the ministers and the chiefs of the armed forces. Here they could play for leisure and utilize their strategic thinking. It was a perfect mix of pleasure, skill and wit.

'I want to reward this man for his invention,' pronounced the king, clapping his hands twice. The treasurer came forward immediately and waited for the king's orders.

The king said to the man, 'Ask away, and we shall fulfil your desire. Do not hesitate, the Gupta Empire is known for its charitable disposition towards the poor, the righteous, the talented and the saintly.'

The humble man, concealing his overjoyed heart, spoke unpretentiously.

'Long live the Gupta Empire, my lord. I will be obliged if you could give me a few grains of rice.'

Unimpressed, the king raised an eyebrow and said, 'A few grains of rice . . .'

'Yes, my lord,' said the man.

'How many kilos?' questioned the king.

'My lord, I'm a man of numbers, so if I may request you to place two grains of rice in the first square, four grains of rice in the second square, eight grains of rice in the third square, sixteen grains of rice in the fourth square and like that in each of the remaining sixty squares of the ashtāpada, that will serve me well.'

The king was ready to grant the chess master's desire, but before he could announce, 'So be it,' the treasurer screamed at the top of his lungs.

'VISHNU! VISHNU! VISHNU!'

Startled by his reaction, everybody turned to look at the treasurer, who rushed to the king's throne.

'My lord, please decline this man's offer and instead give him some few dozen servants, some tracts of land, some bags of gold coins, some boxes of precious jewels and one milk cow with her calf,' whispered the treasurer in the king's ear.

'That's too much of a reward for a game,' the king said, a little angrily.

'My lord, we won't be able to fulfil what he has asked for and the good name of the Gupta Empire will be forever tainted,' warned the treasurer.

'By the time we reach the sixty-fourth square of the ashtāpada, we would require eighteen, followed by eighteen zeros, rice grains, to keep our promise to him. We'd never be able to grow and reward so much rice in our entire lifetime,' the treasurer explained humbly.

> *jyeṣṭhatvam janmanā naiva, gunairjeṣṭatva ucyate*
> *guṇāt gurutvamāyāti, dugdhaṁ dadhi ghṛta kramāt*

Friends, this interesting verse explains that simply by having access to better resources that come from birth, money or contacts, one cannot expect to have excellence in life. It is just like when milk gets transformed into curd and then into ghee, gradually gaining mass, increasing in its value and attracting a higher price. Greatness is acquired by personally walking the path of virtue, by cultivating our God-given intelligence and by putting to good use what we have.

MAKING GHEE AND SELF-IMPROVEMENT

The first step to self-improvement is to *adopt the right culture*. Just as milk turns into curd in association of yogurt culture. The journey to greatness begins by adopting a culture of discipline. This is the first stage and requires upgrading to better habits and mental attitudes. A winner's temperament is available in the association of those who are advanced in the subject that we wish to master.

Next, we have to *begin the hard work* of churning our mind and intelligence, just like curd is churned till it separates into butter and buttermilk. This preparation stage requires patience, tolerance against undertaking monotonous tasks and a keen learning observation. The more we invest in preparing, the better we will shine while performing.

Finally, we have to be prepared to *face the heat* of challenges, obstacles and dealing with our limitations, just like butter is heated till it comes to a boil and then left to continue boiling on a low flame until all the residual water is boiled away and the golden ghee finally appears. This is the commitment to excellence stage. Excellence in any field requires consistent effort with determination despite the odds by engaging all that we have learnt and cultivated.

This quote is attributed to the famous Albert Einstein: 'No problem can be solved from the same level of consciousness that created it.' If we really want a solution to all our problems, whether individual, collective or global, then we must work to elevate our consciousness before we can approach a well-rounded solution.

By transformation of our consciousness through the practice of authentic spirituality, we can incrementally begin to develop our abilities. By adding meditation on the Supreme Lord, we can deeply transform our consciousness beyond what other mundane approaches can offer. We can then win over all internal and external challenges through this higher level of consciousness as pointed out by Albert Einstein.

POWER OF SMALL IMPROVEMENTS OVER A LONG TIME

Many people, in their enthusiasm to improve, make wonderful New Year's resolutions. They may pay large annual gym subscriptions at the start of the year or declare to their parents, partners and teachers that they will no longer waste time, etc., etc.

But promises of bringing about big changes in yourself overnight are hard to keep. *Do not underestimate the power of small incremental changes and progress.* Over a period of time, just like the sixty-four squares on the chessboard, a multiplier effect on the number of grains, our small incremental improvement sums up to big gains. Even on the spiritual journey, a small but honest endeavour to elevate our consciousness will have a multiplier effect on our overall personality and perspective in life.

Therefore, let us be focused, faithful and thoughtful of the Lord and wait for the tremendous, intense transformative effect of spirituality on our consciousness.

THOSE WHO DEDICATE THEMSELVES TO SELF-IMPROVEMENT DEMONSTRATE THE FOLLOWING TRAITS:

1. **Harmony** between their purpose, passion and profession.
2. **Resilience** in the midst of adversity.
3. **Integrity** in character.
4. **Dedication** to service without selfish consideration.
5. **Self-Confidence** in their mission.
6. **A Conservative Nature** in choosing their intimate associates.

THIRTEEN

Overcoming an Inferiority Complex

Human Quality: Inferiority

Makrant Khosla was starting a new job as a business development representative for a private bank. His plump face with thick eyebrows, a broad nose and small eyes looked cheerful when he smiled. Bubbly by nature, Makrant looked at challenges as opportunities. 'I'm bold and carry a "just do it!" attitude,' Makrant had confidently replied when he was asked about his biggest strength during the interview. After various assessments by the Human Resources team, Makrant had been selected for his positive approach in life.

During the eight weeks' extensive training at the bank's Training Centre in Chandigarh, Makrant had learnt a lot. He now knew a great deal about the banking products he would be selling, legal and company policies, system navigation and other technical aspects of the job.

After six weeks of in-depth product training, it was the two weeks of soft skills training that Makrant had really been waiting for. 'How do customer conversations work? How do we pitch and position a product? How do we handle objections and close a deal?' were on Makrant's 'Top Skills to Master List'. The dreaded ghost of public speaking had to be captured within two weeks and Makrant's fear of it had to retire.

Ranjan Sharma, the group's soft skills trainer, had an optimistic and helpful personality. 'Be original, learn the concepts of selling. Don't try to spill out a sales script; you will never be a great salesman like that. Understand the people you are speaking with, identify their needs and think in terms of how your offering can best help them. Then you will not sound like a robot. Rather, you will naturally get the right words to use and your conviction will leave a mark on the customer,' said an emotive Ranjan during one of the sessions.

During the session on 'Opening a Conversation', Ranjan emphasized the value of a strong opening. 'To be frankly honest, I've spent the most inspiring time of my life in the arms of a woman who is not my wife!' exclaimed Ranjan as everyone's ears perked up on hearing this admission by their innocent-looking teacher. 'It is her love and inspiration that drives me further and I'm sure you too have someone like that in your life. My mother inspired me as a child and continues to do so even now,' he added, to calm the gossiping minds of his audience.

'You see how my use of words immediately captured your imagination . . . this is how you must think creatively while opening your presentation,' he concluded.

Based on his training performance, Makrant was deployed at the Jalandhar branch of the bank. He was excited and nervous. On the first day at his base branch, the branch manager engaged Makrant in a practice role play. Makrant was to present a mutual fund product to his senior colleague Shweta, who was a top saleswoman. Shweta had been instructed to test his product knowledge and his rebuttal handling skills.

Makrant had to put into practice all he had learnt during his training in his inaugural pitch to his senior colleague. The training room was packed and the branch was to open for the day in twenty minutes. An audience of fifteen colleagues, his reporting manager's presence, the top saleswoman to test him, the time crunch and the heavy chole-bhature-lassi breakfast that Makrant should really have avoided were all acting in the moment of truth.

Suddenly, Makrant went blank. Not sure where to begin, he started thinking backwards. As Shweta introduced herself as a prospective banking customer, Makrant blurted out:

'Madam, the best years of my life were spent in the arms of a lady who is not my wife . . .'

Aghast to hear what she just did, the middle-aged Shweta looked at the young Makrant with eyes wide open and a dropping jaw. Looking at the horror on Shweta's face, Makrant quickly tried to recover.

'What I mean to say is that I've spent the most inspiring time of my life in the arms of a woman who is not my wife . . . But, but, but I can't remember who that lady was . . .' said a confused Makrant sheepishly.

ārabhyate na khan vighnabhayen neechaih,
ārabhya vighnavihitā viramanto madhyāh
vighnaih punah punarapi pratihanya mānāh,
prārabhya cottamajanā na parityajanti

This nice verse presents a winner's mindset as follows:

> Most people avoid taking the uphill walk to self-improvement by hiding their fears and inabilities behind excuses.
>
> Others desiring to win in life start off with gusto, but give up when they run into obstacles. They talk more about their problems as if these obstacles were trophies. These trophies decorate the display counter of their mind and they don't grow tired advertising these to collect sympathy medals.
>
> The winners, however, even after being beaten, even after tasting no success despite honest endeavours, maintain a bigger vision of their goal instead of their problems. They are committed to humility and therefore remain undeterred from achieving their goals despite all roadblocks.

Lord Caitanya has declared humility as our most empowering and most unfailing friend. He has said:

> *tṛṇād api sunīcena, taror eva sahiṣṇunā*
> *amāninā mānadena, kīrtanīyaḥ sadā hariḥ*

He says here that each one of us must cultivate humility like a blade of grass and harness tolerance like that of a tree. A blade of grass is trampled upon, but it rises again, albeit slowly. It bends as per the force of the foot that steps on it. It does not maintain arrogant rigidity like a stick, which would get it totally crushed. Humility and tolerance in the face of failures and challenges open a world of opportunities for us:

- Rather than dishonestly hiding behind excuses, humility to admit our shortcomings prepares us to gather the determination to overcome them.
- Humility to accept our goof-ups, our mistakes or circumstances beyond our control helps us to maintain the focus on our goals. We can then review, amend, adapt and modify our approach to try again.
- In the face of defeat, humility acts like our shield and protects us from exploding in resentment or imploding in depression. It protects us from becoming hopeless or feeling helpless.
- And finally, in victory, humility keeps us grounded and not go wayward, becoming intoxicated by success.

God has uniquely gifted each one of us. Let us not live in inferiority or superiority complexes. Rather, let us cultivate humility to identify and put to good use the gifts we have been granted by the Lord.

FOURTEEN

Honesty Wins

Human Quality: Honesty

King Vishwanath Singh Randev of Rajpura did not have a successor. He was very worried about the future of the kingdom. Without a well-trained ruler, how could the state affairs run smoothly and without corruption? Being wise when it came to gaining counsel, the king consulted his Prime Minister Jayant and shared his worries.

Jayant replied to the king, 'My lord, the recommendation of dharma shastras in a situation where no good options are available is to first adopt a mood of detached action, *nishkaam-karma-yoga*. Such detachment frees the mind and intelligence from the gloom of not having the expected. Then with such a liberated mindset, one can work towards building more viable options. Let us try to find a worthy candidate, train him or her up and ensure a bright future for Rajpura.'

'What must be the criteria for us to shortlist the prospective candidates?' asked the king thoughtfully.

'Your majesty, for any role of responsibility or leadership, the utmost criteria are honesty, courage and selflessness,' responded the prime minister.

The king discussed a plan he thought could work to find a suitable candidate and the minister kicked into action as per the king's recommendations.

The next day, a statewide announcement was made:

'Our motherland of Rajpura is looking for her future leader. Towards this end, kids between the ages of eight and twelve are invited to attend a special event at the Raja Ji House. This exclusive event is only for children. It will be personally hosted by His Majesty Sawai Vishwanath Singh Randev this Sunday morning.'

With the news of the king looking for his heir apparent, the metropolis was buzzing with excitement. The kids were excited to be allowed into the royal estate and the parents with the prospects of their child becoming the future leader.

On the event day, the king personally offered breakfast to a large gathering of boys and girls. After giving them a tour of the palace and narrating briefly the history of the predecessor leaders, everyone assembled at Rani Maa Gardens.

'Boys and girls, thank you for coming and giving a fresh breath of life to the palace. As a memento, all of you will now be given a special pot, a water flask and some seeds to grow a plant. In six months' time we will meet again for a bigger event than today's. We will then check the growth of your plant to score your progress for our future consideration. Do not take any elder's help in growing your seeds,' announced the king.

The children went away and got into action with dedication and excitement. At the end of the six months, they all assembled again at the palace with their prized plant trophies in hand. Eight-year-old Gitanjali's plant 'Akaash' was the tallest, Sardul's plant 'Bheema' was short and looked like a bull's horn, Ratan's 'Dilbaag Singh' had beautiful purple and pink flowers, and Sarita's plant 'Annapurna' had freshly growing okras hanging. Like this, everyone's plant had special features.

Nine-year-old Prithvi, however, one of the youngest participants, stood alone with an empty pot.

'Your majesty, all year I have been trying. I first got a book on gardening from my gurukul's library. I read it and tried following the instructions as far as I could understand. I *treated the seeds with a thin layer of cow urine* to coat them with some natural disinfectant first. Then I aired the soil to ensure my seeds had the best home to live in. Next, I mixed the best cow dung manure to ensure there was sufficient fertilizer available for the soil to feed my plant. I would water it only after checking the soil and ensured it got sufficient sunlight. I protected it from weather attacks and pests who wanted to make it their home. But this "Gopu" did not wake up from sleep!' explained an animated Prithvi.

'Most kids have admitted that they took help from their parents to grow their plants. Tell me boy, did you not consult anyone?' asked the king in a deep and concerned voice.

'My dad insisted on helping me. He even mentioned our neighbour Sardul's Bheema growing "big and stout" and my Gopu losing to him. But I informed him that we had been asked not to allow elders to help us. I don't know why he was upset with me. He often made fun of my sleeping Gopu, but when my Maa spoke with him, he stopped annoying us,' replied Prithvi.

Post a special lunch buffet, the kids were asked to assemble again in Rani Maa Gardens. The king made an announcement to an assembly attended by all the kids, the ministers and important members of society.

'Boys and girls, thank you for all your efforts. Each and every one of you had such interesting stories. Your plants have now been transferred to be part of this royal orchard. We have chosen one of you to be trained to become the future leader of Rajpura. Please join your hands in welcoming your future king, Prince Prithvi Raj Singh Rathore!'

Surprised by the king's choice, the kids spoke in hushed tones.

'Is the king all right, Prithvi's seed did not even grow . . .'

'His Gopu got scared seeing my Bheema and never came out!'

'No, no, Prithvi is too stupid to know what to do; my dad was saying that even his own father had no hope in him.'

'The king does not know how to value real talent.'

These were some of the things being said.

After a small felicitation ceremony where Prithvi was attired in royal garments, the king addressed the assembly again.

'My dear citizens, many of you seem to be surprised by our choice of your future king. Let me explain what we were looking for and how we measured all of you on those criteria.

'The seeds given to you were actually roasted and they could not have germinated and fructified! So, all of you failed the first and foremost HONESTY TEST.

'Next, most of you admitted already that you took "a little help" from your parents. Some of you have admitted that you purchased a new plant from a gardener. And some of you who did not take help from others have still, under the influences of others, changed your seed to grow a plant. Only Prithvi passed the COURAGE TEST as he did not succumb to his father's insisting or peer pressure.

'Thirdly, only Prithvi passed the SELFLESSNESS TEST by continuing to take care of a hopeless situation without any scope of results. He did not stop attending to the responsibility given to him and looked after the pot throughout the year.'

satyameva jayate nānṛtaṁ
satyena panthā vitato devayānaḥ
yenākramanty ṛṣayo hyāptakāmā
yatra tat satyasya paramaṁ nidhānam
(Mundaka Upanishad 3.1.6)

This is a famous verse which contains the national motto of India, 'Satyameva Jayate'. This verse reinforces the place of truth and honesty in our lives. It explains that ultimately, it is truth alone that triumphs. By truth alone all paths are illuminated; all learning is based on truthful transmission of knowledge. Progress on the path of perfection by the wise, who have all their desires fulfilled, is made possible only when an honest effort has been made and not by inaction or excuses. And by truth alone can one reach the abode of the supreme perfection, the two lotus feet of the omniscient Lord.

NICE GUYS FINISH LAST?

'You will be taken advantage of if you are honest, nice and humble' is a common misnomer against being humble.

However, you don't have to be crooked to make your way forward in life.

Friends, there is a big difference between being nice and being naive. Being simple and being stupid are also two different things. Similarly, we don't have to be humiliated for being humble.

Noble virtues are not a weakness. Rather, they are the pillars of a fair society, a stable family and a responsible individual. They allow us to stand for freedom, equality and love. Wars happen over lies and greed, while peace is made over promises and mutual consideration.

LIFE AND BEING NICE

The sorrows of life require a brave heart. But the brave need not be bullies, from going through the rough and tumble of life. We must find inner strength, which comes from actively cultivating higher values.

The Gita lists many wonderful qualities to cultivate for a successful material life and a progressive spiritual life. To reiterate, to be nice doesn't mean to be naive; it means to be free from different vices. Vices like lust, anger and greed may provide us fleeting pleasures, but are deemed to be gateways to a miserable life.

Ultimately, scriptures point out that being nice means to adhere to dharma or one's roles and responsibilities. And while doing the right thing, it helps to also be polite and courteous.

FIFTEEN

Gossip Passes the Karma too

Human Quality: Verbal Austerity

A powerful yogi lived alone in the forest and practised mystic yoga. He subsisted by begging once every three days. He would come to the adjoining villages and beg for alms from whoever he saw first.

Once, having fasted for three days, the yogi was walking out of the forest and saw the king of the province riding high on his beautiful Kathiawari horse. As per his practice, the yogi extended his begging bowl in the king's direction and asked for alms. The king, however, was crooked in nature and asked one of his soldiers to pick up some horse dung and put it in the yogi's begging bowl. Without protest, the yogi turned back to enter the forest again.

A few months later, the king was out hunting in the forest. He suddenly saw a huge mountain of what looked like horse poop. Alarmed, he thought of a large enemy army camping there in preparation of an attack on his kingdom.

Investigating quietly, the king came across a mystic sitting in meditation.

'Hey, you!' yelled the king.

Disturbed, the yogi slowly opened his eyes and seeing the king who had insulted him, he said, 'I see, it's you, welcome.'

'Do I know you? Where has this huge hill of horse dung come from? Is there any enemy camp coming around for military drills?' the king asked many questions at a time.

'Yes, you know me. In fact, you gave me the charity of horse stool in my begging bowl,' replied the yogi.

'Well, dear king, understand this, whatever is given in charity to a worthy person grows like the arrow of Lord Rama; nobody can check it,' he said.

Worried, the king asked, 'When will this poop hill stop growing?'

Looking away, the yogi replied, 'It will not stop, it will keep growing until it submerges your entire kingdom.'

Immediately, the worried king jumped off his horse and understanding his offence towards a genuine mystic, begged forgiveness.

'Please forgive me for my impudence, I accept my mistake and beg your pardon, O saint. Please advise me what I should do to stop this calamity.'

'The religious codes in dharma shastras explain that when someone gossips about the wrong done by others, they become party to the offence. So, to mitigate this horse poop offence, if others talk ill about you, then and only then can the situation be thwarted,' explained the mystic.

Apologizing and offering prostrated respects to the jungle mystic, the king departed with his permission.

That night, the shrewd king devised a plan. He asked his priest to come the next morning and bring his daughter along.

'I want to talk to you and my daughter wants to catch up with your daughter,' he proposed to the priest.

The next day, the priest complied and came over with his daughter to the king's palace. By the afternoon, the king sent back the priest after harmlessly mentioning his horse poop charity given to the mystic.

'Since the two girls are still busy chatting, I will send back your daughter before sunset in the royal palanquin guarded by my soldiers,' he assured the priest as he sent him back alone.

By evening, the priest became anxious and, unsure about the whereabouts of his daughter, came running to the palace. He was stopped by the guards who had been instructed by the king to do so. The king had also asked his daughter to keep the priest's daughter busy and serve her as her own younger sister.

The priest, now full of doubt about the king's intentions, cried from pillar to post and ill-mouthed the king to many people of influence in the kingdom.

'I cannot believe that the king would kidnap the daughter of his priest. What else can be expected of a man who gives horse poop in charity to a mendicant!' people whispered, gossiping about the king.

The next day, the king sent the priest's daughter back accompanied by his own daughter and with many gorgeous gifts of silken dresses and gold jewellery. As instructed, the princess publicly hugged the priest's daughter and invited her to visit the palace again. The priest now realized his mistake, but kept everything to himself about the false accusation, fearing repercussions.

Then the king left to check the forest site and found that all but one small piece of horse dung was left behind.

Paying his respects to the yogi, he explained what he had devised and how clearly it had worked. People gossiped about him and became a party to the offence hanging on his head.

'But I am worried about this last bit of horse poop. How come this remained?' he asked.

'There is someone in your kingdom who never engages in gossip-mongering. She is an old lady who makes clay pots, earns an honest living, never accepts money that she hasn't worked for and never tells a lie,' said the great mystic.

Taking his leave and disguising himself as a civilian, the king found out about the old lady and went to her hut as she was making some mud utensils.

'O mother, why are you toiling alone, let me help you,' said the disguised king.

'Thank you, but I'll be all right,' replied the old lady politely.

'No, no, you are like my mother and I will help you,' he insisted.

'I told you dear sir, I do not need any help at the moment,' retorted the old lady again, respectfully.

Desiring to somehow engage with her and then drag her into some gossip to nullify the last remaining piece of horse dung, the king tried many tricks.

At last the old lady, although irritated by this uninvited assistant, said assertively in a monotone with the grave facial expression of a school headmaster, 'I know that you are the king of our province in disguise.'

Thunderstruck, the king asked, 'How did you find out?'

The old lady revealed the secret of her ability to know people's hearts.

'I never lie or cheat. Because of this, God has given me the ability to understand those who try to lie to and cheat me.'

Turning close to the king's ear, the old lady whispered with a smirk on her wrinkled face, 'And you know what dear king . . . that last piece of horse dung, you might have to eat it if you want to get rid of it. I am not going to ever bad-mouth you or anybody else!'

paravācyeṣu nipuṇaḥ sarvo bhavati sarvadā
ātmavācyam na jānāti jānānapi vimuhyati

Friends, this wise verse points out the negative tendency of finding and advertising the faults and shortcomings of others. The verse further exposes the double standards we sometimes adopt when we liberally overlook our own shortcomings. Displaying generous tolerance towards our own faults and mistakes, we hesitate to do the same for others.

The sages have pointed out the weakness of the ear. The ear finds pleasure in:

- Hearing the faults and mistakes committed by others
- Hearing our own glorification even if false

ADDRESSING DISPARITIES WITHOUT DESPISING

The Gita gives us many practical instructions to overcome a petty mindset. It states that the noble-hearted are averse to finding faults in others (Bhagavad Gita, Chapter 16, Verse 2). They would rather spend their keen observation in self-reflection to take responsibility for self-improvement.

They don't appoint themselves as public correction officers and do not hold the weakness of others against them. In a nutshell, they focus primarily on seeing good and doing good, for themselves and for others.

When the need to point out a fault genuinely arises, the mature-hearted employ 'verbal austerity' (*vāṅ-mayaṁ tapa*; Bhagavad Gita, Chapter 17, Verse 5). They make a conscious effort to speak the truth of the matter, but in a manner that is affectionate, helpful and not unsettling at the receiver's end.

In pointing out a mistake or in correcting a negative situation, their purpose is not to make others feel bad, but to benefit them. On how that situation could be addressed better, they give honest feedback that is communicated positively and politely. It is not ego or fault-finding, but genuine goodwill for the betterment of others expressed respectfully.

In contrast to these characteristics of the noble-hearted, the unscrupulous are plagued with ungodly qualities. Slaves of ego, they revel in violence—in speech, in plans and sometimes even in actions (Bhagavad Gita, Chapter 16, Verse 4). Riding the high horse of self-righteousness, they gratify the sword of their tongue by cutting deep with vicious speech. When hungry for more, they eat burgers made from horse poop patties of gossip and rumour-mongering. They are champions of the blame game and turn lying into an art form.

Friends, let us curb these negative tendencies for fault-finding, criticism and gossip by engaging the tongue positively in glorifying the Lord. Likewise, by hearing about His all-perfect character, we can check the ear's negative tendencies. It is only with the positive engagement of the tongue and ear that we can leave no room for negativity.

SIXTEEN

Do You Want to Become the Most Powerful?

Human Quality: Satisfaction

Om Ratan was born in a family of stone artisans. His father, uncles and grandfather were all proud stonecutters, but being the youngest, Om was unsure about taking up the respected, rewarding but tedious profession of an artisan. In secret, he was considering different career paths.

'Omi, the magnificently carved fort of the king and the antique beauty of the queens' palaces narrate the centuries-old story of the art and skill of us artisans,' said a persuasive Shiv Ratan, Om's elder brother.

'And the fine dirt of red stone that gave Baba bad lungs is also the legacy of the same magnificence,' retorted Om in a disapproving tone.

'Omi, you are being unduly critical of our profession. It has fed our family and brought us the king's recognition. Do you really want to retire from the family occupation for a teacher's job at the local school?' asked Shiv in a penetrating tone.

'I am not sure what I want to do,' responded Om as he walked away.

During the same week, Giriraj Das, a travelling monk, was passing through Om's hometown. He spoke at an event where Om was in the audience. There was something simple, yet magical, about the monk, Om thought. He decided to approach him and ask him about his dilemma regarding what career to follow.

'Om, every man is responsible for his own choices. We feel suffocated when others decide what we do with our life. In the Gita it is said that one must take up a profession according to one's psycho-physical nature. A profession mismatched to your personality will cause frequent burnouts, boredom or undue stress that will negatively affect the quality of your life,' advised Giriraj.

'What do you reckon I should do?' asked Om Ratan.

Giriraj said, 'Think deeply about your personality, observe and work hard on a range of things to find what your core strengths are. Then look for an occupation that best suits your temperament. This way, you will be engaged in doing what you love and therefore excel in your work since you will love what you are doing.

'Why don't you take a year between stone carving and what you want to do next? The universe is a university and it is teaching us who we are and what we are meant to do with our life.'

Giriraj invited Om to join him for a tour through Rajasthan. Om accepted hesitantly, but felt that this was a golden opportunity to learn more about himself.

On the first leg of their trip, while in Udaipur, Om saw a wealthy businessman. Draped in rich silks, white jodhpurs and a multicoloured turban studded with a gold brooch, the man walked with his head held high, as his servant carried a large umbrella overhead.

'He's the famous owner of the big cloth house . . . see how regal he looks,' said someone in the crowd.

'Maybe I should start a business venture . . . "Om Ratan Wedding Silks". I can become rich and famous like this man,' said Om to his new travel mate.

But Giriraj advised him not to make choices purely based on monetary considerations.

'Don't try to imitate a successful person's career by only looking at their success. You must understand their situation and your own nature first. Your path may not be theirs; a decision driven by greed is a dangerous way to choose. A career path and an occupation are not only meant to earn you a living, but also to bring you inner wealth. In the absence of inner satisfaction, even if you become successful and earn a lot of money, you may employ that money in harmful ways to fulfil a deeper lack within.'

Om understood the underlying principle of fulfilment through engagement as the key to worldly success and inner prosperity. As a remembrance for the lesson, he carved a small elephant out of Udaipur's famous white marble.

Jaisalmer was next on their trip. While Giriraj went to pay respects at Vyas Chhatri, Om joined him to catch the iconic city views from the top. On their way back, they saw a big procession with state guards on horses, accompanying soldiers, musicians and an announcer. It was the state collector on revenue services. Carried in an official palanquin, the influence and power of the chief revenue officer was on full display. As the announcer called out names one after the other, big businessmen came, paid their respects and presented their business ledgers. Some even paid taxes and fines there and then.

'What if I prepare and become a big government officer? My influence will be greater than others' affluence . . .' he shared with Giriraj.

'Again, it will be the same mistake as before. Choosing a career simply on social considerations will not embed the values within you that are required to undertake such a profession. Power corrupts. Unless you are deeply grounded in values like integrity, selfless dedication and bold honesty, you will be tempted or trampled. You won't find inner peace through work simply on account of official respect.'

Om understood the underlying principle of work as a means of executing one's inner values, and the danger of getting wealth or power without such values. Again, as a souvenir, he carved a small replica of Vyas Chhatri out of Jaisalmer's famous yellow marble.

A month later, while in the lawns of the beautiful Radha Govinda Temple in Jaipur, Om spoke his heart out to his new best friend, Giriraj.

'These past few months have been instrumental in my life. Thank you for sharing your wisdom with me,' said an appreciative Om Ratan.

'I am simply sharing the Gita's wisdom on choosing an occupation. It is explained there that everyone has a unique personality type. Some are intellectual, some are administrators, others are business-oriented and still others are service-oriented. The Gita explains that any type of these persons can attain perfection in life by simply engaging in their own natural deeds, like a business-oriented person running a business or an intellectual taking up a teaching role.'

'What if we chose an occupation that does not suit our personality?' asked Om.

'When people undertake work which is in sync with their psycho-physical nature and in a spirit of worshipping the Supreme, then that occupational engagement becomes a means for perfection,' explained Giriraj.

'On the contrary, if artists were to adopt administrative roles, they would certainly not get the platform for self-expression in a disciplined formal environment. They will feel suffocated even though they are earning well. Similarly, attracted by money, if a service-oriented personality were to run a business, he or she may lack the risk-taking courage that is more abundantly available to someone with a resourceful business-oriented personality,' elaborated Giriraj.

'So, what do you think you are inclined to do?' he asked Om.

'I am amazed at how practical the Gita's approach is to finding out what you want to do in life. First, understand yourself, your inner nature, then position yourself in a career path accordingly. With reflection and observation, I certainly find that I have a need for public recognition. I want to leave my signature on the canvas of time. I don't think I can work in an office or in a position taking orders. I am pretty hands-on active and of an independent nature. Basically, I am an artist at heart. My brother's persuading me had turned me away. But I'd like to set up my own artisan studio. Nothing else will fulfil my heart as much as an opportunity to carve dreams out of stones,' said Om Ratan with a confident smile.

śreyān sva-dharmo viguṇaḥ
para-dharmāt sv-anuṣṭhitāt
sva-dharme nidhanaṁ śreyaḥ
para-dharmo bhayāvahaḥ

In this verse of the Gita, adherence to our duty has been emphasized. It is being said here that often we can feel repulsion about undertaking our ordained duties due to their tedious or 'non-attractive' appearance. We may not feel driven by our own occupation in the presence of the glamorous occupations of others. This verse, however, explains that our own duties always lead us to the best long-term outcomes. In fact, it is being said here that sticking to our own duty, however burdensome it may appear, never leads to any misfortune. (Bhagavad Gita 18.46)

FIND YOURSELF AND BE YOURSELF

The Gita recommends that we act according to our own natural duty (*sva-dharma*) and not to indiscriminately pursue deeds and duties suitable for someone else (*para-dharma*). Attracted by affluence, position or the popularity of others, we may try to tread their path. But we should not forget that one man's food can be another man's poison.

Trying to be someone else is as good as throwing away our own treasure for the sake of someone else's dream. The only things we gain are low self-esteem and an overall inferiority complex.

Our natural duties are determined by our own natural abilities and activities. We should work on identifying and further cultivating them. Engaging our natural abilities with work suitable to express them will ensure that our inner nature and outer occupation are in sync. Such harmony between our temperaments and occupation brings inner fulfilment, which is the foundation of a peaceful life.

SEVENTEEN

Leadership Means Integrity

Human Quality: Integrity

Vishnugupta, famously known as Chanakya, is credited for making a statesman out of a non-royal, ordinary citizen. Known for his sharp wit, foresightedness and uncompromising discipline, Chanakya's integrity was perhaps his most prominent character trait.

Once, a Chinese scholar came to India to study its culture and its leaders. Wherever he went in India, he heard about the daring exploits of Chanakya. Glorified as a clever teacher of ethics, a proponent of meritocracy, an ace economist, a thoughtful jurist and a brilliant political adviser, Chanakya captured the imagination of the Chinese intellectual. The Chinese scholar decided to travel to Patliputra and meet the mastermind behind the Mauryan Empire.

After a long journey, the scholar finally reached the palace of the king, but was surprised to learn that the great Chanakya never accepted a royal residence. The guards pointed him to the location of Chanakya's hut. They forewarned him not to take any gifts or try to appeal to Chanakya for any political favours.

'Is this where the top politician of your empire stays?' asked the surprised scholar to the palace guard who had been sent to escort the foreign guest to Chanakya's residence.

'This hut is so small and the entrance is tiny,' he said.

'Yes, this is where the revered Chanakya stays. The door is kept small to invoke humility, as state heads, including his own king, who come to meet him, have to bow to enter,' responded the guard.

The guard entered the hut and after bowing, said, 'Revered prime minister, a Chinese scholar has travelled far to have an audience with you. It's late evening already, shall he be allowed now or shall we advise him of a later time more suitable to you?'

'He's already here and must be tired travelling. Never make guests wait for you; it's disrespectful to the person and unpleasant for the relationship. Please send in the foreign guest,' replied Chanakya.

Once inside, the Chinese scholar saw that the hut was almost empty. There was a straw mat for sleeping faced eastwards, a small table with another sitting mat for work in the northern corner, a small water pot and two more sitting mats for guests and a small doorless bamboo closet for the meagre belongings of the first minister of the Mauryan Empire. There were no utensils or other furniture in the hut.

Chanakya asked his guest what language he'd be comfortable conversing in and quickly adopted the dialect of his scholarly guest's choice. Before the pleasantries could get over, Chanakya lit a lamp near the water pot and doused the one on his work desk. He came back to his desk again and the two wise men started conversing.

'I see that you have turned off this lamp while turning on that other lamp in the corner. Yet you have come to sit here at your desk again. Is there a reason for that?' asked the keenly observant scholar.

'Well, I understood from your honourable mentions that you have not come to see me in an official capacity, but in a personal capacity. When you entered the hut, I was doing some official work, but not any longer. Therefore, I have doused the lamp for which the oil is paid for by the state and have lit the one for which I pay.

'Sitting at this desk, I still represent my state, but in a personal capacity. I understand our talks are going to be of a personal nature and although they will have nothing to do with the king and his work, sitting at this desk obliges me to hold dear my allegiance to my king. Therefore, I want to maintain complete transparency and have an honest exchange of dialogue with you,' explained Chanakya.

vivekah sah sampatyā,
vinayo vidyayā sah
prabhutvam prakshayobhedam
cinham etan mahātmanām

This profound verse says that one need not take down a giant to be known as a great person. Real greatness in people can be recognized when the riches of their character increase. This is demonstrated when:

- One possesses wealth without losing discretion.
- One grows in learning while growing in humility.

- One's power or influence is exercised with politeness and with a helpful temperament.

UPTIGHT, NO. ENLIGHTENED, YES

Chanakya is famous for his integrity. But often he's portrayed as a ruthless wise man. Does that mean you need to be cold and stone-hearted to be a person of integrity? Not quite. A strong moral compass is not to judge others, but to conduct oneself with honesty based on consistent standards. Clear and consistent principle-based living does not have to reduce a virtuous person to a robot.

The Gita enlightens us that our values are based on our knowledge. What we know decides what we value. For example, one who has never seen a car manufactured by Ferrari does not know of its luxury design and race-inspired performance. Such a person is going to be perfectly content in acquiring a local made car with a basic design and performance, even if they have the resources to buy a Ferrari. Therefore, our knowledge base decides our values, and from our values we make decisions.

By investing our time to acquire different types of knowledge, especially spiritual knowledge, we can come to better understand our selves, the world and the relationship between them. With spiritual wisdom, we can truly expand our worldview and benefit our character with higher values of compassion, tolerance, wisdom, inclusiveness and integrity. Such virtues prepare us to face the hard knocks of life and temptations of the world, and overcome the challenges posed by our own mind.

While bold, unapologetic executors of their values may often claim to be people of strong integrity, Gita wisdom points out that without humility and compassion, all other values can feed our egos in the wrong way.

By cultivating higher knowledge, we can bring synergy between our thoughts, words and actions. Then we can reshape our lives to become like the authentic people who we adore and admire. Integrity in character is the foundation for winning the trust of others and trust is the currency for leadership.

Let us commit ourselves to living by higher values through the cultivation of higher knowledge. Only then we ourselves and the world around us become better.

EIGHTEEN

The Gift of Patience

Human Quality: Sense Control

Dushyant was the only son of a wealthy businessman who lived in a remote village in India. Earlier in his life, Dushyant had made friends with people without really understanding their true character. Attracted by their popular social ambience and mesmerized by the alluring calls of their style and clothes, Dushyant held these spoilt wealthy kids on a pedestal. Anxious to be accepted by them and be as popular, Dushyant had inadvertently subscribed to their whims, styles and habits.

The power of association quickly had its effect on Dushyant. To keep up with his 'friends', Dushyant had adopted their mindsets. With extravagant spending habits, dressing opulently and living as if for an audience, Dushyant was fully aping his heroes. As one bad habit often leads to another, Dushyant's narcissistic need for self-importance and social superiority over others saw him lose many good friends often due to judging them externally.

Surrounded by ego-smitten competitors or adoring free-riders, Dushyant had no good counsel left in life. His pleasure-seeking saw him burn away his inheritance on luxuries and parties. His alcohol indulgence eventually drove him into poverty. Once poor, he was discarded by the free-riders and made fun of by his competitors. Empty-pocketed Dushyant was eventually alone.

In the days of yore, he had shown some interest in learning the art of pottery. Back then, Dushyant was in his prime and life offered him endless possibilities. He had learnt basic pottery skills with the dream of building a ceramics business in the future. Regrettably, his bright future was ruined by his indiscriminate choices and undisciplined habits.

One day, Dushyant found an old and broken potter's wheel in the village junkyard. Tears of happiness and agony ran down his face as visions of his lost dream of owning an art studio raced through his mind. Dragging the potter's wheel to the slum where he now lived, Dushyant set it up. With no one to help, his poverty-stricken arms could hardly spin the wheel. For love or money, pottery was his only hope for relief from the harsh reality of what had become of him. Dushyant would amuse himself, toying with his broken potter's wheel, lost in imaginations of art and glory.

Once, Dushyant made some mud ready and crafted a pot in small instalments of spinning the wheel. Due to the lack of proper spinning, the pot came out strange like a flat-based football elongated at the top like the beak of a flamingo. In short, it looked odd. Dushyant burnt some dry foliage to bake his work and used whatever unused paint he had to put a layer on top. Once dried, he took his weird creation to the city in the hope of a sale.

'Wow! I've never seen a vase like this. That's so avant-garde,' someone commented, looking at the pot.

Whether joking or serious, the comment ignited Dushyant's dreams. However, he wasn't sure what to tell the lady when asked for its price. She had offered two silver coins to Dushyant, but he declined. The mud exhibit triggered emotions of excitement and value that had long been lost in him.

Returning back to his thatched hut without making a sale, and with a handful of begged flat-rice, Dushyant hung the pot in a bag hooked in the roof. He kept looking at the pot as if he had found a long-lost friend while eating his begged handful of rice-flakes. The words 'That's so avant-garde' kept resounding in him as he tried to sleep, still gazing at the pot hanging from the ceiling.

Once asleep, Dushyant heard a voice.

'Dushyant, I am very impressed by this piece of art. This form has been unseen by the human eye ever before, its raw texture, the fire-burn effect on its colour and its ash glaze finish are all a very unique mix of a refined sense of aesthetics. Here are one hundred gold coins; this masterpiece *belongs* in the royal court.' The reward and honour given by the king in the dream made the sleeping Dushyant very happy.

The dream evolved and soon Dushyant had intelligently invested the one hundred gold coins to set up his ceramics studio, bought a new potter's wheel, one that spun with a pulley, and hired an assistant to operate the pulley as he busied himself producing artefacts, one after another.

Dushyant was not only rich in this dream, but famous. With each pot selling for hundreds of gold coins, Dushyant was soon taking orders from the aristocracy. Soon his name spread throughout the country and consignment orders were coming from foreign lands. The king of Jammu personally came to see Dushyant's gallery. While there, the king's beautiful daughter had expressed her desire to marry Dushyant, to which the king had rejoiced.

Now married to an exquisite Himalayan princess, dreaming Dushyant had to hire security to guard his palatial bungalow. The couple went for exquisite holidays in South India, to see the Lord's elephants in the famous Guruvayur temple. Upon returning to his house, Dushyant received a royal honour from the king of his province.

Often, our long-cherished desires and deep resting fears take shape in dreams. Dushyant's dream evolved further and the couple had three handsome sons. All of them were well-behaved and obedient. But as they grew up, they fell in bad company. Dushyant tried to guide them from his own experience, still accessible to him in his dreaming state, but fame and money had spoiled the boys already.

The dream then turned into a family drama.

To teach a lesson to his younger sons, Dushyant stopped his eldest from going to a party. The father and son had an argument which made the mother cry. Pacifying his wife and chastising his sons, Dushyant ordered that they be grounded for a week. The eldest son rebelled and there ensued a tussle for freedom. Both father and son yelled and screamed at each other as the servants watched in sympathy for the father.

Impressions from the many cruel things that had been said to Dushyant in real life made their way into the dream with his imagined son becoming an agency of insults.

At one point, the spoilt rebellious son said something very objectionable about Dushyant's past and the father lost it completely. He picked up the golden mace that was awarded to him in honour of his service and chased the unruly son out of his bungalow.

The mace in his dream was actually his walking stick in the real world. Dushyant had picked it up while now sleepwalking!

With his golden mace in his hand and his eyes fixed on his beautiful wife, Dushyant spun the mace one last time to declare to his fleeing son that severe punishment awaited him should he not mend his ways.

But outside the dream in the real world, the swinging stick in the hand of Dushyant landed on the unsold mess of a pot hanging from the roof. The pot smashed out of the bag and landed on Dushyant, breaking his dream and his forehead.

viṣayendriya-saṁyogād
yat tad agre 'mṛtopamam
pariṇāme viṣam iva
tat sukhaṁ rājasaṁ smṛtam

In the eighteenth chapter of the Gita, Lord Krishna points out the nature of three kinds of happiness available in the world (Gita 18.36). We can experience uplifting happiness through the cultivation of goodness, enticing but unfulfilling happiness through passion and degrading undesirable happiness through acting out of ignorance. In the verse presented above (Gita, 18.38), the nature of happiness in passion has been explained. Such passionate happiness is derived from sensual contact; it tastes like nectar to begin with, but ends up like poison at the end.

THE ROOT CAUSE BEHIND OUR MISERY

As mentioned earlier, the Gita explains that we are fundamentally spiritual beings—indestructible souls seeking everlasting joy. Our current home, the material world with all its various pleasures, is temporary by nature. It cannot cater permanent pleasure to us. Our seeking of pleasure is not the problem—that is our natural need since pleasure-seeking is the innate nature of the soul. The problem is our choosing to seek pleasure in temporary material objects instead of their permanent spiritual source, God or Krishna.

The quality of happiness the eternal soul seeks is also eternal in nature. But when that need is engaged for fulfilment with temporary material objects, all we experience is fleeting happiness with a lasting thirst for satisfaction and a restless anguish caused by frustration. The soul's attempt to draw happiness through material objects is the root cause of its ongoing misery in the world.

MATERIAL MEANS TO SPIRITUAL NEEDS

Consider Dushyant or addicts like him, say to alcohol, or drugs, or pornography or junk food. Before they became addicted, they were probably leading normal lives, but being pleasure-seeking in their core spiritual identity, they started indulging in material objects that titillated their senses. As a result, they kept drinking, or doing drugs, or watching porn or eating fast food. Over time, their cravings became compulsive and addictive, leaving them dysfunctional and distressed. Such cravings can even degrade them, impelling them to do immoral or even illegal things. But essentially, such troubles grew out of their search for pleasure.

The Gita teaches us that in the material world the pleasure-seeking spiritual soul is covered by a material body and operated by a material mind. Thus, the body-mind unit is only the external covering of the real us, the soul.

The best means to find lasting happiness in the material world is through the cultivation of goodness within us. This is achieved by stilling our external material-self and coming into contact with our blissful inner spiritual-self. When we focus on connecting with God or Krishna by adopting the science of bhakti-yoga, the resulting spiritualization of our consciousness helps us relish the fulfilment that we were craving unnecessarily in worldly objects.

NINETEEN

Fool's Friendship Is Fatal

Human Quality: Self-Discipline

One time a guru, Pragyabodh (literally, 'learnt through discrimination'), and his disciple, Chanchal Iccha ('wandering desires'), were travelling. They came to a strange country called Sapnapur ('dreamland') ruled by King Budhiheen ('bereft of knowledge'). In Sapnapur, everything was unbelievable. By the order of King Budhiheen, everything was being sold at one rupee per kilo, be it gold or cotton.

While passing through Sapnapur's busy streets, the young disciple Chanchal Iccha saw that all the sweets were being sold at one rupee a kilo. Overjoyed, he requested his guru to settle for good in Sapnapur.

'Guruji, for a mere one rupee I will be able to eat all the sweets I want!' he exclaimed.

'No, we should leave this place immediately. The offers here are too good to believe. This enticement will certainly trap us in dangers unseen at the present,' warned Pragyabodh.

Mesmerized by the prospects of enjoyment in Sapnapur, Chanchal disregarded the warnings of his wise mentor.

'Be wary of cheap thrills, Chanchal. The king here is obviously a fool to enforce such a stupid policy. Do not stick around here for long,' the master repeated with emphasis.

But with his mind dreaming of cheap sweets, Chanchal had fallen in love with Sapnapur. In no time at all, he put on weight overeating all those sweets.

One day, a villager's goat jumped on a compound wall, the wall fell down and the goat was crushed. The villager came to King Budhiheen and petitioned, 'My dear king, there is such injustice happening in your kingdom.'

'What happened?' asked the king.

'Well, my goat was standing on the neighbour's wall which fell and my goat died. I want justice!'

True to his name, the foolish king said, 'Justice shall be done. The wall must be punished. We shall hang the wall.'

The envious villager exclaimed, 'The wall also died when it fell. You can no longer hang it. You have to hang the neighbour.'

To this, the king responded, 'Okay, hang the neighbour.'

The next day, the neighbour was summoned. King Budhiheen did not try to investigate and simply asserted, 'It was your wall that fell and killed the goat; we will hang you in punishment.'

The smart neighbour knew exactly how to rescue himself from the stupidity of his king. He said, 'O king! I have no role to play in it. It was the mason who had built the wall.'

The king summoned the mason, 'Call the mason, we will hang him.'

Then the mason was called to the open court where the king was passing orders and delivering 'justice'.

The mason dodged the unfair punishment by passing on the blame.

'My lord, once my tailor had accidentally poked one of my eyes with a needle. Since then, I can only see with one eye. It is because of the tailor's mistake that the wall I built was a little off. And therefore the real culprit is the tailor.'

Unsurprisingly, now the tailor was summoned.

King Budhiheen asked the tailor, 'Why did you poke the mason's eye with your needle? Because of your mistake, an innocent goat died. We will hang you as a punishment.'

The tailor was also an expert at passing the buck. He replied, 'My wise king, it was not me who poked the eye. It was the needle! Since the needle was made by the blacksmith, it's the blacksmith's responsibility.'

The king now summoned the blacksmith.

'We are going to hang you!' ordered the king.

Horrified, the blacksmith asked, 'But what did I do?'

The king explained, 'It was you who made that needle and that needle was in the tailor's hand and that needle poked the mason's eye and the mason made a faulty wall and the wall fell on the goat who died. So therefore, you're responsible.'

The blacksmith was bewildered as the king announced the hanging to be conducted in fifteen days.

Out of fear and depression, the blacksmith did not eat anything for fifteen days. As a result, he lost a considerable amount of weight. On the day of hanging when the hangman tried to put the noose around the blacksmith's neck, the noose was too loose and wouldn't fit.

The king's minister said, 'My lord, the rope's noose is too loose and doesn't fit the blacksmith's neck. Shall we pardon him in this case?'

To this the king objected, 'No! Have you taken a bribe from the blacksmith? Everybody has gathered here to see justice prevail in Sapnapur. Find somebody who is plump and whose neck will fit the noose or we will hang you.'

Searching fervently, the minister saw Chanchal who was eating some milk sweets while watching the hanging ceremony. He was arrested and brought to the podium where the hangman put the noose around his neck.

At that point, Chanchal started crying and repenting, 'Oh! My dear guru had warned me not to stay in Sapnapur and not to overindulge in the cheap thrills of this place. I wish he was here to rescue me.'

Seeing Chanchal in danger, Pragyabodh immediately appeared at the site. He conveyed something to Chanchal in sign language and then proceeded towards the king.

'My dear king, do not hang this foolish Chanchal, hang me instead. I am his guru and ultimately, I was meant to control him. So the responsibility was mine, I failed at it and therefore, I'm the right candidate for punishment,' said Pragya.

Surprised to find the first willing candidate to be hanged, the king asked, 'What you have said makes sense, but I am yet to be convinced. Why do you want to be hanged?'

In response, Pragyabodh said, 'Actually, this is the perfect time to die. Whoever dies at this moment, at this muhurta, will become the emperor of the whole world in the next life. And therefore, I want to die right now.'

The king stood up and in a protesting voice said, 'What the hell is going on in Sapnapur? Such an auspicious moment and nobody informed me. I will not allow you or your disciple to die. I want to be hanged so that I die at this auspicious moment. Indeed, I am the only suitable candidate to become the king of the whole world in the next life.' And in this way, both false attraction and stupidity are won over by wise discretion.

> śraddhāvāl labhate jñānaṁ
> tat-paraḥ saṁyatendriyaḥ
> jñānaṁ labdhvā parāṁ śāntim
> acireṇādhigacchati
> (Bhagavad Gita 4.39)

The Gita verse above tells us the importance of cultivating wisdom and discretion to deal with harmful temptations and unchecked desires. We have to be faithful to cultivating spiritual wisdom if at all we want to reach the supreme spiritual peace. There is nothing superior to spiritual wisdom since it fosters a clearer vision of reality and frees us from our own lower nature.

While no one has a monopoly on wisdom, an honest open-minded approach to observing the world around us will expose the lack of wisdom we have in the world. Despite the brilliant people around us, the global state of affairs shows that our existence is in the doldrums. The ecological, social and personal states of well-being have plummeted. There are large-scale ecological crises threatening humankind, unprecedented depression plaguing human spirits and major social breakdowns dividing humanity. The Gita points out to the root cause of all this—ignorance of our common spiritual nature.

CHOOSE THE INSIDE-OUT APPROACH

Between thoughtless naivety and useless cynicism lies the courage to trust. The Gita explains that by understanding and realizing our spiritual nature, we can go beyond all forms of destructive selfishness.

The Gita is not a book of commandments. It is a book of choices. To change our state of affairs, the Gita strongly recommends that we must look inwards first. We must fix our inner world before we venture outwards.

A famous American novelist has said, 'People do not wish to appear foolish; to avoid the appearance of foolishness, they are willing to remain fools.' Therefore, since we are all gifted by God with the virtue of intelligence, we must now cultivate the right discrimination (*pragya-bodh*). But how can we do this? By accessing higher knowledge available in wisdom texts like the Bhagavad Gita. Otherwise, we will remain enslaved to our sensual desires (*chanchal iccha*) and perpetually suffer in the cycle of rebirth in this land of false promises, the material world (Sapnapur).

DEALING WITH CHEAP THRILLS

The Gita presents a clear path of the psychological journey that leads us to the pitfalls while we try to enjoy the world. By identifying the different stages of temptation, we can achieve real peace and real happiness in life.

All temptations begin with thoughts. At this *Thought Stage*, we become tempted and begin to ponder over our desired objects or experiences.

Magnified by the mind, such thoughts trigger emotions and cravings within us. This *Emotional State* is identified by feelings of restlessness and longing. We daydream as if our happiness is dependent on attainment of that object or fulfilment of that experience, even if immoral.

Emotions grow into intentions. This *Intention State* sees us lost in our fantasies. We become convinced that what we seek is not what we want but what we need. Thus, we make the decision to get into action. This state is marked by irresistible passion and galvanized thoughts.

Intentions graduate when we act out our plans. The final *Action State* sees us execute our desires and act on our intentions.

The loop of allurement persuasion begins with thoughts, evolves into emotions, proceeds into intentions and completes with our action. All forms of advertising are used to sell us things we don't need at extravagant prices by alluring us into such loops of temptation.

The Gita points out that breaking free and winning over temptations is achieved by the cultivation of *discrimination* and *determination*. The Gita recommends the positive path of bhakti-yoga as the means to cultivate wisdom of ourselves and the world around us. Practices like mantra-meditation bring us self-awareness and put us in direct connection with God or Krishna, bringing us strength to free ourselves through a higher sense of joy.

TWENTY

Comforting the Distressed

Human Quality: Service Attitude

Anurag, a young entrepreneur, ran his own IT networking firm, ColdWire Networks, in Lucknow. He had recently won the contract for upgrading the network of a government hospital. Late one evening, Anurag was visiting the hospital to conduct a survey for the installation of the new network. He was advised to start at night to avoid the daytime rush at the hospital.

After completing his site survey for all other floors at the hospital, Anurag approached the department for the terminally ill at the fourth floor. Before entering the ward, the security staff gave him an infection control kit to wear. The mandatory boot covers, hand gloves, face mask, hair net and a visitor's gown covered Anurag from head to toe. Meanwhile, the guard noted Anurag's details from his driver's licence in the visitors' record book and placed a sticker with Anurag's full name on the gown he was now wearing.

Anurag entered the ward carrying his tool suitcase. As soon as he entered, Taarini, a visibly anxious nurse, identified him by his name tag and took him to the bedside of a very old patient who was murmuring in pain.

'Jugal Kishore ji, O Pandey uncle, look who is here! You have been asking for him for three days and now when he is here, you have decided to take a nap?'

The sister dragged a chair for Anurag to sit right next to Mr Pandey, who looked to be in considerable pain. Mr Pandey slowly turned towards his visitor and Anurag noticed the various bandages covering the patient at many places on his arms.

Looking at the masked person in the chair, squinting to see more clearly, Mr Pandey extended his fragile and shaky hand towards Anurag. Taking note of the 'Ram' tattoo shining brightly on the old man's oily skin, Anurag held his hand gently. A wrinkled smile appeared on Mr Pandey's face as he held the gloved hand with the meagre strength he had.

'Where were you for the past few days? I was longing to see you,' said Mr Pandey in a sickly tone.

'Baba, I was interstate for work. I am sorry I got late. I flew in only this morning dropping everything just to be with you,' responded Anurag.

Groaning, Jugal asked, 'When do you fly back?'

'I am here now, Baba. Don't worry. We'll go back together. They are all waiting for you.'

Offering him comforting words, Anurag kept expressing gratitude to Mr Pandey, who kept gazing at his face with a gentle smile.

Hours later, still clutching Anurag's hand, Jugal spoke, 'I'm afraid.'

'Of what, Baba?'

'When time will stop on me. Death. The end. No more,' Jugal responded in broken breaths.

'How silly! Death is nothing but a new start, Baba. Remember what Daadu taught us. Death is when our body is left behind, but we move on. The body ends, but the soul is eternal. It is deathless and fearless,' said Anurag reassuringly.

Pacified, Jugal nodded in agreement, 'Yes, how could I forget that. Bhagavad Gita . . . Yada Hi Dharmasya . . .'

Throughout the night they both kept speaking like that. Whenever Mr Pandey groaned in pain or expressed his fears, Anurag comforted him gently with his hand and with spiritual truths that seemed to transcend the gloomy environment of the ward. During her shift, Taarini had requested Anurag to take breaks and catch some rest, but he would politely decline every time, unwilling to leave Jugal's bedside.

Early in the morning, Jugal died peacefully in his sleep. Anurag called Taarini who was just finishing her night shift over and asked her to make the necessary arrangements.

Offering condolences, Taarini said, 'I'm sorry for your loss.'

But Anurag asked, 'Who was he?'

'What! What do you mean?' exclaimed the shocked nurse. 'Anurag Pandey? Are you not Mr Jugal Kishore Pandey's son?'

'No, I am not his son. I didn't know him,' replied Anurag.

'I came to the hospital for my own work to carry out a site survey of your ward. The guard at the door gave me this PPE kit to wear before entering,' Anurag explained further.

'You brought me to this old gentleman's bedside and I realized he was passing away and was simply waiting for his son in his last moments. I'm grateful I was able to serve him and comfort him when he needed it the most,' concluded Anurag.

tapyante loka-tāpena
sādhavaḥ prāyaśo janāḥ
paramārādhanaṁ tad dhi
puruṣasyākhilātmanaḥ
(Srimad Bhagavatam 8.7.44)

This verse explains that great souls have a characteristic feature: they go through pain themselves to relieve the pain of others. The best process for worshipping the Supreme Lord is through selfless devotional service to Him. Once we have cultivated a selfless heart, service to God's creation is then a practical demonstration of our spiritual advancement.

We should therefore engage our lives in relieving the distress of others, especially by sharing spiritual knowledge of wisdom texts like the Gita. Helping to reinstate everyone in their eternal spiritual position of peace, stability and joy is the highest form of welfare work we can render in this world.

WHY SHOULD WE GIVE?

If nature dictates the survival of the fittest, why do we find people risking their own safety to care for and serve others? What makes people sign up for jobs like firefighters where you have to risk your own life to save helpless victims of fire? What inspires the frontline staff at hospitals to not change career paths and continue to care for the victims of a highly contagious pandemic? What is it that makes people go against the natural urge for survival?

Yoga texts like the Gita explain that it is the higher values in us that inspire us to help others, even at our own expense.

While our human nature dictates survival to get us through life, our spiritual nature inspires us to seek something higher above and beyond survival. It is this seeking of a higher sense of worth in life that finds its fulfilment in values like sacrifice, charity, compassion and selfless service.

WHAT INSPIRES US TO GIVE?

Vedic wisdom tells us that we spirit souls are parts of the supreme spiritual whole, God or Krishna. As eternal souls presently in the material world, we are on a multi-life journey of spiritual evolution. By working towards the elevation of our consciousness, we rise higher to more aware and spiritually evolved species and stages of life.

When we finally become humans, where our awareness is greater than all other animal, aquatic or plant species, we cherish higher values like sacrifice and feel inspired to not merely live for ourselves. Thus, as spiritually progressive beings, we are meant to help each other not just to go through life's challenges, but also evolve spiritually until we can attain spiritual perfection.

WHAT SHOULD WE GIVE?

Given the inevitability of our demise and rebirth of our soul in another suitable body after death, we should all work towards making each other's lives as hopeful as they can be for the present and fruitful for the future.

It goes without saying therefore, that a well-evolved human being thoughtfully extends help to the needy. Spiritually developed persons, however, do not limit sharing their worldly assets of abilities and resources for the benefit of others. They understand that the struggle of the eternal spirit soul in the limiting material confinement of the body is the root of all our problems. They are thus focused on discovering and nourishing others' potential for spiritual growth.

Yoga literature puts the gift of wisdom as the highest type of charity. Such wisdom transforms us into the best versions of ourselves and helps us become agents of positive change. By then sharing the non-sectarian universal wisdom of spiritual truths, as found in wisdom texts like the Gita, we address not just the cyclic problems of life, but also the culmination of all perfections by breaking free from the repeated cycle of birth and death altogether. Reviving our dormant love for God and enabling others to do so is then the most desired gift of freedom to give.

HOW SHOULD WE GIVE?

Through spiritual knowledge and practices, we come to develop as dynamic and determined individuals fit enough to conquer our own demons like lust, anger, greed, selfishness, laziness, etc. It is said that our best intentions can be our worst enemy. The act of giving, especially that of sharing spiritual knowledge, requires us to be selfless, tolerant, pride-less and respecting of others' choices.

A humble and learned heart, not hungry for recognition and self-aggrandizement, is the perfect well-wisher of the world and does not hesitate to make a contribution, howsoever little it may be appreciated or acknowledged.

TWENTY-ONE

Getting Out of the Prison

Human Quality: Repentance

Maharaj Jayasimha had won the kingdom of Swarnabhumi after defeating the tyrant King Rudraveer. Known for his righteous and compassionate justice, King Jayasimha reviewed the prison system of the newly acquired territory and had a meeting with his council of ministers.

'Crime exploded in Swarnabhumi while Rudraveer was busy enjoying royal pleasures. I can't understand how there are hundreds of people imprisoned in Swarnabhumi. Also, Rudraveer was known to punish people out of vengeance. I fear there may be many cases of moral injustice,' said Jayasimha.

'Yes, Rudraveer was a cruel king. He levied heavy taxes and disproportionate punishments. He was irresponsible and many people turned to crime during his extended vacations,' informed a minister, nodding in agreement with King Jayasimha.

'I want to reassess all the cases of those who are serving life sentences for non-violent crimes. Based on the nature of the crime and the duration of the jail term already served,

I want to review who can be safely released on probation to integrate back into civil society,' explained Jayasimha.

The ministers organized a visit to the jail for the new king. One by one, many inmates were brought in front of the king as he questioned them while reviewing their jail records.

'For what crime are you serving a life sentence here?' asked King Jayasimha asked the first inmate.

'Maharaj, I am innocent. The property crime case against me was crafted by my neighbour. His family bribed the judge and here is an innocent man standing before you seeking justice,' said the inmate.

'Hmm . . . send his papers to the review panel,' directed the king to the minister of justice.

The next inmate was a short man with a round face sporting a thick beard.

'Maharaj, the case of organized fraud against me is bogus. My business partners cheated not only me, but also our investors. They had high connections in the king's palace and all of the blame was put on me. They are enjoying the spoils of the fraud they committed while an innocent man like me is kept in jail,' said the inmate.

'Hmm . . . we'll review your case and criminal history to see why a life sentence was awarded to you. You may leave,' said the king.

The next inmate was then brought in front of the king.

'Maharaj, I know this is not the first time I am here. I got into a life of crime due to fate's injustice. But I became reformed, learning it the hard way. The case of drug trafficking against me is made up by that rich merchant. I have found out that the judge who gave the verdict against me had a share of the profits from that drug deal case I was caught for. I am innocent and the real criminals are roaming free!'

'I want to see you transformed and contributing positively to society when you are released from here. Thank you for coming,' said the king, looking at the inmate.

'It seems Rudraveer wanted to create the fear of punishment to prevent crime. At best, fear may repress the wrongdoers, but it is insufficient to inspire inner transformation. Without higher values, people will commit crime despite stringent laws, as it is evident here in Swarnabhumi,' whispered the king to his minister who sat close to him.

'Next . . .' said the king, turning to the jail guard.

Another inmate serving life imprisonment for burglary was then brought in front of the council.

'I see your file and find that you have committed many petty thefts in your life. For what crime are you serving life imprisonment now?' asked the king.

'Maharaj, I am a victim of a judgemental society. I committed a small theft once and was labelled a thief for life. I could not find a regular job and I had no land to cultivate either. A long prison life had a criminogenic effect on me, leading me from one crime to another. In the last instance, I was caught breaking-in at the Swarnabhumi Reserve for Currency and Stamps. King Rudraveer was annoyed by my repeated crimes and gave me a life sentence,' said the lean-faced inmate.

'I hope you are helping other young criminals by sharing your experience and the consequences of criminal life. Thank you for coming,' said the king.

The last inmate for the day was then brought in front of the king.

'For what crime are you serving a life sentence here?' asked one of the ministers.

'Sir, I am guilty. I made a wrong decision in life and committed a crime. I am here for I deserve it,' said the man, looking at the ground.

'What did you do?' asked the king.

'It was fifteen years ago, when I was a teenager. My father was a soldier in the king's army and he died fighting on the frontlines. I was given employment at the palace kitchen in lieu of my father's service and my mother was given a state pension. One day, on the king's wedding anniversary, a special feast was prepared. After the event was over, I saved some of the pudding I loved in an earthen pot to take home for my mother. I was accused by the chef and charged with stealing. Since the pudding was covered in real gold flakes, the gravity of my crime was held equivalent to stealing gold from the palace. I was awarded a life sentence,' explained the man.

Upon inquiring more about this inmate, the king found out that he was very well-behaved, helpful to the prison staff and an avid reader of spiritual texts.

'What is the best thing that you have learnt at the prison?' asked the king.

The inmate replied, 'About ten years ago, the now retired jail warden had organized a Freedom Festival at the jail. Some monks visited us and taught us essential spiritual truths from the Gita. We learnt that our real self is the soul held captive by the judgement of karma within the confinement of the body.

The body itself is housed in the jail of the material world, held captive by the forces of nature. Nobody is free here.'

'How was all this information useful to you?' asked the king.

'Well, ever since then, I have been working on freeing myself from the duality of selfish desire and repulsion, basically from attraction and hatred. The Gita taught me that we act wrongly either out of uncontrolled desires or out of hatred and envy for others. I started conducting myself more responsibly. The monks' joke that "Fortune may favour the brave, but karma never discriminates" stayed with me. Without taking responsibility for our life occurrences, it's hard to make the best use of whatever life may offer us.'

The king asked further, 'You are jailed and have limited capacity to act and interact. How did this knowledge help you practically?'

'Hmm . . . firstly, my depression went away. I was relieved from the burden of hopelessness by nurturing my spirituality. I also became free from the hatred I felt for others. I no longer hold others responsible for my situation,' said the inmate.

Clearing his throat, the king responded, 'Everyone else we've met today held someone else responsible for their mistakes—relatives, neighbours, business partners, fate and the world around. You are the only one sincerely accepting your mistake, even though it was an unjust punishment for a minor fault.'

'Maharaj, the injury of injustice never begins to heal until we learn to forgive—others, as well as ourselves,' responded the inmate.

Pleased, the king said, 'I am ordering your release and placing you under the mentorship of our current jail warden as an employed correction officer. I am sorry that you spent fifteen years for a minor mistake. I hope you can share your wisdom with other inmates and help bring about personal transformation in them.'

> *dhruvaṁ tato me kṛta-deva-helanād*
> *duratyayaṁ vyasanaṁ nāti-dīrghāt*
> *tad astu kāmaṁ hy agha-niṣkṛtāya me*
> *yathā na kuryāṁ punar evam addhā*

Friends, this verse is a reflection from a repentant heart. An arrogant son of a priest gave capital punishment to the noble king Parikshit for a minor offence. Instead of blaming the boy, hiding behind excuses or retaliating, the king accepted the unavoidable as the verdict of fate.

From this verse we can see how King Parikshit understands that neglecting the injunctions of the Supreme left him vulnerable to make such a mistake. This triggered the punishment inflicted upon him. King Parikshit then takes responsibility for the consequences of his mistake, expresses gratitude for the punishment as a means to become free from the reactions to his unfortunate behaviour and finally, he resolves not to commit the same mistake again.

Repentance has a constructive role to play in our life. The five features of repentance are:

Regret: feeling remorse for the mistake or for our role in the mistake.

Responsibility: taking personal accountability and reviewing our intentions.

Recognize: acknowledging the consequences of our mistake.

Regard: expressing gratitude to those who extend us help to change and reform.

Resolve: not relapsing to old ways and being determined to continue on the path of transformation.

TWENTY-TWO

The Cup or the Juice

Human Quality: Detachment

Professor Vijay Gopikesh headed the department of computer science engineering at the reputed Institute for Internet Technologies, Bangalore. He was known for his experiential teaching methodologies and treated his students as his peers, as his children and as his responsibility. His coding classes were as packed as a cinema on the release of a popular movie. Often staying up all night helping weak students prepare during their exams, Prof. Gopikesh was as much loved by the students as by their parents. He travelled interstate every alternative weekend to conduct free teaching classes for the less privileged students. He also donated all the royalties he earned from his published books for funding spiritual educational projects. These were commitments that kept the professor away from his own family. A special recognition from the Ministry of Education was given to him for his dedication to the student community.

During an interstate tour over the weekend, the professor invited a special group of recent graduates to the hall of his host engineering college. The set-up was interesting; on the projector screen, there was an animation of a two-headed demon swinging many weapons in his multiple hands. The demon stood on a broad pavement of what looked like a chain of black boxes with random white spots.

In one corner of the hall, there were trays with some refreshments. The hall was empty and the chairs had been piled up at the back. There were cushions spread out on the floor and light kirtan music played in the background. Around a dozen guests of his special group arrived and made themselves comfortable, although reluctantly, on the cushions on the floor. These students were those who had no luck during campus placements and were now having a tough time finding employment.

The professor welcomed his career-struggling guests with his oceanic smile.

'How are you all?' he asked everyone to a dull response from his audience.

'See that table over there with so many drinks? Go on, grab one and come back here.'

For every student, there were many different options of mocktails, soft drinks and fresh juices to choose from. Each beverage was in a different drinkware and a straw flag had the drink's name printed on it. With the drink down and the kirtan music gently picking up, the group felt more relaxed and now open for conversation.

'Mukul Rastogi, tell me, what's happening?' asked Professor Gopikesh with verve.

'Not much, sir . . . still no calls. I have applied for so many roles. It feels like job hunting is my full-time unpaid job. All I'm getting calls for are totally hopeless contract roles,' came the response.

'Ok. How's the drink? Which one did you pick?' asked the professor.

'Ya, it's lovely . . . it's the citrus peach cooler.'

'Madam Neha Kamboj, what's the gossip?' asked the professor, turning to another student in the group.

'The gossip has gone cold, sir, still no calls. The market has such harsh starting requirements in order for us freshers to be considered,' replied Neha, disenchanted.

'But at least your drink is chilled. Which one did you choose?' asked the professor.

'It's now my new favourite, pomegranate mint magic,' Neha replied.

Turning to another student on the floor, the professor asked gently, 'Jai Shri Krishna Kinjal, beta. How are you?'

'Jai Shri Krishna, sir, I'm very sad. I worked very hard and got such good grades, but now everyone is rejecting me due to a lack of experience. I am a recent graduate. You tell me, where do I bring experience from?' said a dejected Kinjal.

'Hmm . . . we'll figure something out. How's your drink and which one is it?' asked the professor, cheering up his student.

'Watermelon blueberry punch . . . it's yummy,' she replied.

And like this, the professor asked each of the students what their job hunt experience had been like so far and what drink they had picked from the trays. Afterwards, he addressed them as a group.

'My dear students, I want you to check the cups you had your beverage in. Do you notice anything?' asked the professor in a thoughtful tone.

'Each one of you has picked the best cup with the most interesting drink in it,' pointed out the experienced teacher.

'The poor old plastic cups, the everyday tumblers and the simple glassware also had the same drinks, but they could not win your attention. Interestingly enough, no one picked the regular cola, plain buttermilk or the good old orange juice, although they were available in both simple and expensive cups,' he completed.

Thus pointing out his observation, the professor said, 'I've seen it over the years; young graduates like you have your eyes fixed on the best and the most exciting. To be honest, it's quite an external view of the world—the glamour, the prestige and the position. However, we often overlook perfectly good options for the sake of the best. Don't let the best become the enemy of the good.

'Many graduates feel they are entitled to a high starting salary based on their grades and expectations of their parents. But we must first be realistic. Without first becoming a valued contributor by gaining enough work experience, how can you expect a six-figure salary?' emphasized the professor.

'Thank you for this interesting thought exercise, Professor, but there seems to be not enough opportunities in the market. There are plenty of contract roles, but not enough permanent jobs,' said Nidhi.

'Jobs are available, beta. The challenge is to find the right fit for you,' responded the professor.

Turning to the projector slide, the professor pressed the slide controller in his hand. One by one, each of the black boxes broke away and stood independently from the 'pavement' they formed upon which the demon figure stood.

'Oh! These are QR codes,' called out Nidhi.

'Yes! And I want you to scan that top one. Visit the website this QR code is linked to. This is a portal for self-paced, self-development learning. If you find your current skills insufficient for the kind of roles you wish to get, upskill yourself.'

'Professor Gopikesh, thank you for always making such endearing efforts for us. My worry is how do I get my phone ringing for interviews?' asked a desperate Mukul.

'Son, you should first stop applying for roles blindly. It's tempting to apply for just any role that comes up online, but employers see that as a lack of career direction.'

Pointing to another QR code, the professor said, 'Mukul, I want you to visit this website. This is for a career coach. Work with them to uncover your values, interests, personality and skills before continuing to blindly hunt for a job. Make sure your career plans are aligned to your personal goals.

'All of you should download the app linked to this next QR code. This app provides industry meet-ups, meetings with career mentors from various industry backgrounds. Build your professional network and find out roles that are not published online. Personal leadership is essential to survive and thrive in today's market,' shared the professor.

Pressing the slide controller while pointing to the demon figure, the professor unveiled the slide title, 'My Inner Cynic'.

'Guys, tame this demon who resides in your minds. Do not disempower yourself by believing in your weaknesses and giving away your power to self-doubt. Remember the Gita's famous advice, '*Karmaṇy evādhikāras te mā phaleṣu kadācana*,' concluded the professor.

karmaṇy evādhikāras te
mā phaleṣu kadācana
mā karma-phala-hetur bhūr
mā te saṅgo 'stv akarmaṇi
(Bhagavad Gita 2.47)

Friends, this famous verse the professor referred to requires us to first understand that we can't control whether our efforts will bear fruit or fail to do so. What we can control is whether or not we try. While results lie beyond our control, this verse shows us that the area of our influence is our efforts. The Gita directs us to concentrate on fulfilling our responsibilities without longing for pleasant results or running away from unpleasant ones.

Such a detached approach to work frees us from fears, distractions and disappointments. From practical experience, we can see that we often subject ourselves to feelings of inferiority and inadequacy when our efforts don't bear fruit. Similarly, feelings of superiority and supremacy can intoxicate us when the results do come. Both these complexes are the two sides of the same ego-coin, while the reality of the matter is that we alone are neither the cause of our success nor of our failure. All we can be in charge of is the commitment to our duty, whether pleasant or otherwise.

'DETACHMENT FROM RESULTS? THEN WHAT WILL MOTIVATE US TO WORK?'

While we are encouraged to work without attachment to results, this idea is often misunderstood. People usually question where they would find the motivation to work if it were not for the results. The Gita's call to be detached from results does not imply detachment from goals. This approach brings our attention to the present.

Results are seen after a task is completed, whereas goals are set before the task is started. So, instead of longing for a desired distant future that we have no control over, we are advised to live and work in the present and bring our focus to the work at hand. Goal-setting is not contrary to the Gita's teachings of detachment from work.

DEALING WITH DISCOURAGEMENT?

Gita wisdom repeatedly lays importance on the inner equanimity of the mind towards both the success or the failure of our actions. This wise attitude towards work helps us get of the rollercoaster of expectations and disappointments. Pleasant and unpleasant duties both are to be carried out with an equal sense of responsibility if at all we want real peace in our life.

A universal fact is that, while we are makers of our destiny, we are never the masters of it. Thus, the Gita asks us not to assume a role beyond our capacity, to avoid discouragement. In the universal scheme of things, we have our role to play. Our happiness in life depends on how well we play our part. Being part of the supreme whole, we minute souls can draw supreme courage and inspiration by recognizing our existential connection with the Supreme Lord.

TWENTY-THREE

Monkeys in the Well

Human Quality: Cooperation

The eastern coast of India is studded with the beautiful Eastern Ghats mountain ranges. Many discontinuous ranges of limestone, iron and igneous rock mountains are spread through northern Odisha and Andhra Pradesh to Tamil Nadu in the south, and also pass through Telangana and Karnataka. There are many prehistoric castles and caves reminding us of the kings and sages who resided there long ago. The sounds of the rivers Godavari, Mahanadi, Krishna and Kaveri have been playing welcome songs for centuries in the Eastern Ghats.

In one of the mountain ranges, high up in the Shevaroy Hills near the city of Salem in Tamil Nadu, a large group of monkeys were thriving in the tree kingdom. The king monkey, Ballu, watched over and guided the clan which had two leaders. Nala, a strong adventurist, had his group of monkeys and Nila, another dashing braveheart, led his group.

Both Nala and Nila were always locked in contest. With Ballu watching over, fights were rare, but the competition was fierce.

'Put aside personal ambitions and work in a spirit of cooperation. There is so much more that we can achieve if it does not matter who gets the credit,' was Ballu's repeated advice to the two monkey groups.

'A community thrives on trust and mutual dependence, but when diseased by self-interest and ego tantrums, everything gets spoiled,' Ballu often warned.

Once, Nila's group found a well deep inside the forest. Surrounded by a high wall of trees, the well was full of sweet water and was surrounded by the abundant fragrance of white lilies.

'This is our well. We will not allow that Null-aaa to take water from it,' said an aggressive Vaayu.

'His name is Nala, not Nullaaa. Be competitive, but maintain respect,' said Nila, instructing his commander.

'We have to bring Master Ballu here. That is the tradition and those who break tradition have an unsure future,' concluded Nila.

Two monkey messengers were then sent back to the camp in the Shevaroy Hills. When Ballu heard about the finding of a water well, he was overjoyed.

'Let's go and check the site. If it serves our purpose, we shall move there permanently,' said Ballu.

'Let that Dheela and group move to their newfound paradise. We will stay here, this is the place of our forefathers,' said Agni.

'Commander Agni, it is not befitting for a monkey of your stature to call your senior by a derogatory name. They would not have found this water if they were slack like you are implying by calling him Dheela,' said Nala in a corrective tone.

'Let us follow Master Ballu's instructions and not create fringes,' said Nala.

With both Nala and Nila's camps alongside, King Ballu inspected the well site. The well was broad, and they tested it for depth by throwing in big boulders.

'The well is very deep and it won't run out of water. It seems to be connected to one of the Goddess Rivers. These tall trees cannot be climbed by lions and with the spread-out branches, there is a clear network to travel in all directions. The vines hanging down the new trees and the aerial roots of the old trees are all very good from a security point of view. This hidden jungle paradise is replete with varieties of fruit, cool shade and fragrant air. I'd stay here for four weeks and then decide whether we all move here permanently,' said Ballu.

Suddenly, old Ballu slipped while walking on the tall well wall and fell deep inside. As chaos ensued, the grandsire monkey struggled to stay afloat.

'Quick, look for some long bamboo sticks, Ballu is good at climbing,' instructed Nala.

'No, grab some thick vines and we'll throw it to Ballu and pull him out,' pronounced Nila.

Wise Ballu, although in danger, could clearly see the competitive one-upmanship, petty power play and ego juices flowing between the rival groups.

'Build a long monkey chain, each one of you hold strongly to the hands of two other monkeys, one on each side. Then climb down into this well with the help of this chain and grab me and pull me out. I am too old to climb a bamboo and won't be able to hold on long to a vine to be pulled out. I need each one of you to cooperate and save my life,' said Ballu, as he struggled to stay afloat.

As the monkey chain formation began, old rivals from both groups were now holding hands. Agni was holding Jeet on one side and Vaayu on the other, both from the rival group. One after another, rivals came together for a common cause. Meanwhile, Ballu started running out of strength to stay afloat, but he was only a few hands away now. Nala held on to Deva, the last monkey in the chain before him. Ballu was still an arm's length away.

Then Nila climbed on to the chain to go down into the well. Nala was the last link in the chain and both rivals had to grip hands for Nila to then grab Ballu.

'Nila, God has gifted you with long arms. Today, they would be put to great use, brother,' said Nala encouragingly.

'Your grip is as strong as a python's. I can fearlessly depend on the strength of your arms, brother Nala,' responded an appreciative Nila.

Finally, Nila grabbed Ballu, who had passed out due to exhaustion. Now, the monkey chain had to push back.

Just then, as the chain was steadily pushing back, one monkey stepped on the foot of another monkey from a rival group.

'Watch where you put your foot!'

'You watch your mouth!'

'Who do you think you are?'

'The one who found this well!'

And like this, an argument ensued between rival monkeys as their leaders tried to pacify them.

Words quickly turned hostile and in a thoughtless move, the monkeys left each other's hands to settle the war of words with fists and jaws. To everyone's peril, the entire monkey chain formation fell into the well and eventually everyone drowned.

> *paraspara virodhe tu*
> *vayaṃ pañca ca te śataṁ*
> *anye sākaṁ virodhe tu*
> *vayam pañcādhikam śataṁ*

Friends, I know this story does not have the happy ending you were expecting, but often, a spirit of competition turns sour in a peer group when the spirit of cooperation is diluted, especially during pressing times. The above verse from the Mahabharata sheds light on how to strike the right balance.

During their exile in the forest, Yudhisthira discovered that his wicked cousin Duryodhana had been captured by a Gandharva tribe. Although Duryodhana always treated the Pandavas as his enemies, at that critical time, Yudhisthira resolved to fight Duryodhana's captors. Yudhisthira secured his release and saved Duryodhana from imminent death. Although always pushed into competition by the Kauravas, the noble Pandavas never lost the vision of the collective good of the larger group, the extended family.

Yudhisthira held that if they were to fight the Kauravas, they were five Pandava brothers against the hundred Kauravas. But for an outside enemy, they were all together and their strength was one hundred and five brothers all united.

PEOPLE OR PROJECTS? GOALS OR VALUES?

Friends, never set a goal without a value associated with that goal. Most conflicts happen due to the absence of a larger vision and lack of higher values. When we work towards goals alone, we are more susceptible to overlooking other people involved and turn blind to the bigger picture. While our goals can be the motivator for our efforts, our values should guide our conscience.

We can work towards that promotion at our office as a goal. However, we should also bear in mind the associated value of integrity. This will not only build our public image, but also our professional character.

Passing a competitive exam while cultivating the value of dedication will prepare us to win for life whether or not we taste success immediately.

The monthly business target can certainly be pursued, but at the same time, we can be protected against unlawful acts by pursuing the value of honesty.

Creating a comfortable future for our family while nurturing the value of compassion will ensure greater social good around us.

Friends, next time we are part of a project—whether personal, official, social, national or international in nature, let the spirit of competition not blind us; rather let us allow an appropriate value to navigate our decisions for the best outcome for all associated.

TWENTY-FOUR

Power of Hearing

Human Quality: Self-Transformation

Dr Ish Sharma was head of orthodontics at the Government Dental College near Old Delhi. Every year, the celebrated doctor conducted a free dental hygiene seminar and dental check-up camps in the months preceding Diwali. This year, the doctor was invited by the government medical colleges in the north-eastern paradise of India. They requested him to cover the Seven Sister States including Arunachal Pradesh, Assam, Meghalaya, Manipur, Mizoram, Nagaland and Tripura. This was Dr Sharma's first visit to these states.

Accompanied by one local student from north India to assist him on the trip, Dr Sharma was excited about meeting the welcoming people from the east of India. Akul Sharma, who accompanied the senior doctor, was an ambitious first-year student. Akul was selected for the trip primarily for his resourceful, problem-solving and dependable nature. Tall, heavily set with a pot belly, donning a beard and wearing round framed spectacles, Akul looked much older than his age. In contrast, Dr Sharma was tall, clean-shaven and, thanks to regular workouts, had an athletic build.

Picked from the Maharaja Bir Bikram Airport in Agartala, the dental duo was taken to the government guest house. They were to be stationed there for the next three days to cover more than half a dozen events. With back-to-back engagements, Akul's job was to assist the set-up for the seminar during the free check-up and treatment camps.

Despite their busy schedule, the natural beauty of the place and warmth of their hosts kept the visitors inspired. Over the next three and a half weeks, the duo covered five states. So far, Dr Sharma had conducted fifteen huge public seminars on good dental hygiene, three seminars on advancement in the field of orthodontics for three medical colleges and had examined over 200 patients assisted by Akul and other local dental students.

'Dr Sharma, I have memorized every single word, all the technical terminologies and the punchlines of your presentation. I bet I can deliver a seminar as good as yours!' boasted Akul the apprentice.

'I am sure you can, Akul. Do you want to switch roles for the next seminar?' asked the senior doctor, amused by the confidence of his young student.

'Are you serious!? I mean, I will totally smash it out of the park, sir. I have watched you deliver the same presentation over a dozen times,' said an excited Akul.

'All right, let me chauffeur you to the next venue as the guest speaker and see how you go. I haven't driven in these hill roads before, so it would be a refreshing change for me as well,' offered the doctor, sharing the sporting spirit of his student.

The next morning, following his driver Bitupon's navigation, Dr Ish Sharma drove 'Doctor' Akul Sharma to the venue. Akul aped Dr Sharma's look. He wore the grey suit he was carrying with a white shirt and shiny black shoes. Excited and a little nervous, Akul went over his presentation slides one final time in the car. His career as a dental surgeon was unofficially starting with a talk on the *'Best practices for good dental health.'*

At the venue, nobody had seen Dr Sharma before and Bitupon had already been instructed by the doctor to stay quiet. As the car pulled up outside the venue, Dr Sharma, wearing Bitupon's driver's hat, got off and ran to open the passenger seat door.

'This is Dr Sharma. He has been very excited about coming to your college. And this is Bitupon Sonowal, Dr Sharma's local assistant,' said Dr Ish, fixing his driver's hat as he spoke. The hosts received their special guest with a fresh bouquet of flowers and generous smiles.

The hall was packed with an eager audience, the stage was set, and the microphone was waiting. Akul got off to a good start using one of Dr Sharma's jokes.

Akul: *Knock, knock.*
Audience: *Who's there?*
Akul: *Dishes.*
Audience: *Dishes, who?*
Akul: *Dishes how I talk shince I losht my teeth!*

While Akul delivered the speech verbatim, Bitupon sat at the back of the hall along with Dr Ish disguised as the car driver. Impressed by his presentation style, Bitupon whispered to the doctor, 'Sir, the kid has nearly replicated your talk with such precision and confidence.' Dr Sharma smiled and winked at Bitupon.

Concluding his presentation, Akul said:

'So my final three take-home points for you are . . .

'Number 1: Remember, it is not sweets alone that rot your teeth . . . As we discussed, tooth decay is caused by an acid-producing bacteria in your mouth. This bacteria feasts on carbohydrates and slowly eats away your tooth enamel. These carbohydrates can be from sugar in your famous local sweets like Madhurjan Thongba or a pack of bhujiya or potato chips or even diet cola.

'Number 2: Brush regularly. Starve the bacteria in your mouth by checking this acid production and plaque build-up. Clearing away food residue stuck between the teeth by regularly brushing keeps acidic teeth demineralization to a minimum.

'And number 3: Avoid frequent snacking between meals. As we discussed, some studies have shown that tooth decay is also related to the frequency of eating. The best practice to adopt is to eat three meals a day and to brush regularly. Snacking may be good for the tongue, but is bad for your oral health.

'I'll close here and see if there are any questions . . .' concluded Akul, almost imitating Dr Ish as he walked close to the edge of the stage.

A hand quickly rose in the audience, as if waiting for the opportunity to speak. A middle-aged lady stood up and waited for the microphone to reach her.

'Thank you, Dr Sharma, for the great talk. It's been a privilege listening to you. My name is Dr Ina Gogoi and I have worked at the Srimanta Hospital as a dentist for four years. I have just opened my own dental clinic in the city earlier this month. My clinic is called Aastha Dental and it is next to the Nataraj cinema,' spoke the member of the audience as if it were an advertisement.

The pompous local dentist asked an extremely esoteric question about 'delayed paraesthesia of the inferior alveolar nerve during surgical removal of wisdom teeth'. Digressing here and there and quoting her own approach to the serious dental issue, Dr Gogoi, still promoting her 'state-of-the-art clinic', let everyone in the audience know that she was highly qualified and experienced.

Stumped by the unexpected question, Akul's face turned red. Moving his tongue over his dry lower lip and taking control of his inner panic, Akul's quick wit kicked into action.

'You must be a great dentist, Dr Ina, but I am very surprised at the trivial question you have asked. Honestly, this is so simple that I will let my driver sitting at the back of the hall come here and answer it for you,' said Akul with a cheeky smile as he rescued himself from an untenable situation.

> *yad yad ācarati śreṣṭhas*
> *tat tad evetaro janaḥ*
> *sa yat pramāṇaṁ kurute*
> *lokas tad anuvartate*

Friends, this verse from the Gita recognizes that people emulate a leader and inevitably follow the standards set by the leader's exemplary conduct (Gita 3.21).

Charles Colton famously said that 'Imitation is the sincerest form of flattery.' We find countless Apple Watch-inspired cheap smartwatches to buy online; somewhere in the past, we may have had a dressing style inspired by our favourite sports or movie star; even our ideas and opinions are formulated as a remix of ideas of leading thinkers, teachers, broadcasters and public intellectuals. No wonder the Gita (3.21) explicitly emphasizes the role of leaders as social torchbearers.

It is natural for us to follow those who have reached where we would like to be ourselves. But bhakti literature explains that in our best interest, we should endeavour for *anukaran* (follow the example) and not limit ourselves to *anusaran* (simply imitate) the leaders around us. To be a great leader, one has to first become a genuine follower.

STRENGTHENING OUR CHARACTER

Shifting our focus from imitating to following gives us a great sense of maturity and sincerity. But to follow the worthy examples of those we honour, we need something more than an inspired heart and a determined head.

The technological age makes everything accessible to us at the click of the mouse. There are ultra-fast weight loss programmes and online courses to learn new skills rapidly. But we find no quick-fix for character weaknesses or any crash-courses to develop strength of character. For that, we need inner purification.

The Gita goes straight to the essence of all issues and the root of all self-improvement. It identifies that we must first gain mastery over our mind. Without mental discipline, we fall back to procrastination, old habits or thoughtless living when the initial inspiration wanes away or when we run into obstacles or are trapped by attractive distractions. With our inability to control our mind and follow good advice, we cannot develop substance in our character or hope to make any significant breakthroughs in our life.

Yoga texts like the Gita emphasize upgrading our minds by following practices like meditation, prayer, pranayama and yoga asanas. By understanding our core spiritual nature and connecting with our Supreme source, we relish a profound non-material fulfilment of heart. It is this fulfilment that makes us resistant to the pressures and allurements that compromise our integrity.

Essentially, with the inner enrichment that comes from genuine spiritual development, moral integrity naturally develops. With this, we move away from a cheap life of imitation and its fake reward of fifteen minutes of fame.

TWENTY-FIVE

How to Invest Time Properly

Human Quality: Prioritization

Once, one of the great saints of Vrindavan was sitting among his disciples in a room behind a temple. He was being interviewed by an intelligent American couple who were on a tour of sacred India.

'Swamiji, you speak about the soul being our real self and the body being its shell. We can see and touch the body, but how can we identify the soul?' asked Jenny.

'Consciousness. This living force that permeates the entire body and makes it function is the energy of the soul. Without the soul and its life force, the body is simply a lump of matter,' responded the saint.

'So life force is the symptom of the soul?' Jenny asked with a curious expression in her eyes.

'Yes. All life forms are existing, growing, thriving, expressing, feeling and desiring due the presence of the soul. Can dead matter think, feel and desire?' asked the saint assertively.

'But isn't life or consciousness a product of biological evolution?' Gordon jumped into the conversation.

'The intractability of the evolution of consciousness is a documented fact in the scientific community. *Science Magazine* celebrated its 125th anniversary in the year 2005. It presented 125 big questions unanswered by science in a special news feature published that year. The first question on that list of unanswered questions was pertaining to the origin of the universe and the second was about the origin of consciousness,' interjected a young disciple of the saint.

'But the theory of evolution is a well-established fact as far as I believe,' Gordon rebutted.

'While plenty of theories are thrown around as if they are facts, hard scientific data is sparse to substantiate them. The claim that consciousness is a product of material evolution is an opinion held by many, but not an established scientific fact. A lot that reaches the common man is simply sophisticated hypotheses presented in scientific garb with interpretations suiting their dearly held views,' replied the disciple.

The saint added to his disciple's point, 'Life comes from life, it can never come from dead matter. The conscious energy of the soul produces different forms and different species of life . . .'

'Did I hear you right? Are you saying that consciousness produces the body and not that the body produces consciousness?' asked Gordon with an unsure but inquisitive expression.

'Yes, have you ever seen a dead thing giving birth to its own kind? Life comes from life,' said the saint with no response from Gordon or Jenny.

'The Gita explains in a very logical way how consciousness in this one lifetime transforms childhood to youth, youth to adulthood and eventually adulthood to old age. Similarly, at the end of the present lifetime, this life force transforms into an entirely new form. Consciousness continually changes its form because it has different types of desires. On the basis of those desires, the soul moves into different forms, different lifetimes and even different species. Life is indestructible. It changes forms, but never ceases to be,' responded the saint.

'It sounds similar to the principle of conservation of energy in physics. That energy doesn't cease to exist, but it constantly changes its form,' added Jenny.

Explained the saint, 'Yes, you can try to understand it like that. Even the elements that make up the body are never destroyed. The *pancha-mahabhoot* or the five great elements—earth, water, fire, air and ether—together constitute the body. They continue to exist even after the body is destroyed by death.

'Wisdom texts explain that while the body undergoes six changes—birth, growth, sustenance, producing by-products, dwindling with disease and annihilation by death—the soul does not undergo such changes. The soul is impervious to material changes since it is unaffected by material forces of the universe.'

'So, if I understand it correctly, the soul and its symptomatic life force helps the body evolve from infancy to adulthood. And death is simply a final change of form at the end of one lifetime where the soul transmigrates to a whole new body. Based on the momentum of its desires from the previous life, the conscious energy of the soul evolves into a new body. It sounds very reasonable, but this whole argument rests on the idea that life cannot be destroyed and you back up this idea by referring to the statements of scriptures. What if I don't believe in scriptures?' Gordon asked with sincerity.

'You are an intelligent young man. Let us consider the matter through logic and careful observation without any reference to scriptures,' said the saint with a gentle smile as he straightened up on his old oakwood stool.

'For argument's sake, let us accept the empiricist theory that life is created at birth and destroyed at death. At birth, we emerge from nothingness and at death, we merge back into nothingness. Even this demonstrates that the life force is eternal,' said the saint, demonstrating his point by moving his hands animatedly like a magician who apparently creates a pigeon out of thin air and then makes it disappear into thin air right in front of everyone's eyes.

'So, by this line of argument, life is constantly being created and then constantly being destroyed over time. "Nothing" becomes "something", which becomes "nothing" again. In the beginning, we were nothing and then we became something and at death, we are back to where we started . . . that something again becomes nothing,' said the saint.

'Once destroyed, how can nothing become something again?' Gordon asked further.

'You are American. During winters in your country, the cold climate produces frozen puddles of water on the street sides. But during the daytime when the sun rises, the ice melts and returns back to its original state of water. Again, when the sun sets and it goes cold, the water turns back into ice. Do you follow me?' the saint asked Gordon.

'Creation is followed by destruction and destruction is followed by creation?' replied Gordon, as if taking a calculated guess.

'Yes, you got it. Birth is followed by death and similarly, death is followed by birth. There is continuous recycling of life energy. The essence of the life force is indestructible, no matter how you look at it,' added the saint.

'Similar to this explanation is the scriptural concept of reincarnation. It's not you, as in your present body, who specifically gets reincarnated, but the essence of you, the indestructible life force within you. The external bodily forms keep changing, but the core being, the soul, continues its journey in this world till it evolves to spiritual perfection through genuine spiritual practices,' concluded the saint.

Suddenly, a monkey hopped into the meeting arena. It grabbed the saint's shoe and went running to sit on a nearby tree. The disciples ran behind the monkey to retrieve the shoe. One disciple took hold of a stick and was about to attack the monkey, as it howled and made faces to defend itself. The sagacious saint immediately called out, 'Wait! This is not the way to deal with the residents of this holy land of Vrindavan.'

The saint asked another disciple to bring him some bananas. He took a banana in his hand tactfully and offered it to the monkey. As the monkey came nearby, the peacemaking started between him and the saint. The saint slowly raised the banana towards the monkey and waited for it to respond. The monkey showed keen but vigilant interest in the offer. The saint slowly raised the banana further and waited for the monkey to reciprocate by bringing the shoe forward.

The monkey, however, was experienced; his very purpose of stealing items was to bargain for food. And he was not going to return it cheaply. The monkey brought the shoe out of the grip of his jaws and towards the saint. The disciples' nervous excitement increased as the distance between the gracious hand of the saint and the notorious hand of the monkey decreased.

In a flash, the monkey grabbed the banana with one hand and also retained the shoe in the other.

'Just see how intelligent the monkey is. He knows the art of negotiation. Can dead material elements ever show signs of intelligence and personality? This is the life force we were talking about!' exclaimed the saint, laughing.

The banana deal took a few rounds and finally, after eating a few bananas, the monkey threw away the shoe and went on his merry way.

Friends, there is well-known verse:

> *āhāra-nidrā-bhaya-maithunaṁ ca*
> *sāmānyam etat paśubhir narāṇām*
> *dharmo hi teṣām adhiko viśeṣo*
> *dharmeṇa hīnāḥ paśubhiḥ samānāḥ*

It is described here that eating, sleeping, mating and defending are things which even animals can do very efficiently. Just as in the case of this monkey; he knew exactly how to find his food, how to negotiate for the food and how to capture the food. He was unrelenting in defending his territory and protecting his interests. These four instincts of eating, sleeping, mating and defending are common to both humans and non-human life species.

THEN WHAT IS THE SPECIAL PREROGATIVE OF HUMAN LIFE?

The human being has been endowed with developed consciousness. Humans are therefore called rational animals. Limiting our rationality for the fulfilment of only these propensities that we share with the animal kingdom is the serious under-utilization of our human advantage.

Of all forms of life, the human opportunity comes with the specific focus on inquiring about the higher principles of existence. A monkey cannot become a scientist or a philosopher.

HOW CAN WE PROPERLY UTILIZE OUR HUMAN POTENTIAL?

We have to learn to prioritize time for the higher goals of life rather than just the four mentioned above. Since even a go-getter needs to know where to go and what to get, we need to first understand what these higher goals could be. By self-reflection, we can come to understand this.

Our primary higher goal is the pursuit of uninterrupted inner fulfilment, happiness. Isn't it interesting that we are all driven to achieve anything in life for the sake of inner fulfilment, whosoever and whatsoever we may attribute that fulfilment to? What is the root of our lack of fulfilment despite our achievements? Ponder upon this deeply.

The Gita describes that just as the part's fulfilment is in union with the whole, our existential fulfilment is found in reunion with the Supreme Person, God or Krishna. It is satisfaction at this spiritual level that enables us to experience the joy of uninterrupted fulfilment despite the limitation or failings of our physical, emotional, intellectual or social needs.

Once we taste the contentment of a loving connection with the divine, we are no longer controlled by our monkey reflexes.

TWENTY-SIX

Mystery of Destiny

Human Quality: Transcendence

King Prasen Veenanath ruled southern India. He had a wise minister named Siddhartha, who was known for his sharp intelligence and devotion to God. Siddhartha had a peculiar habit of relating everything that would come to pass as a blessing of the Lord.

'It's the grace of the Lord!' the minister would often be heard reiterating, whether something good or bad happened.

The king was often unamused by the minister's catchphrase. When the king had won a decisive battle by deploying a strategic military force, the minister had congratulated the king while repeating, 'It's the grace of the Lord.' Upon the birth of their twins, the minister had used the same phrase to congratulate the king and the queen. When a foreign scholar was defeated in a public debate by the minister, he had used the same words acknowledging everyone's praise of him.

Once, during a forest operation to capture a wild leopard, the king lost the thumb on his left hand. King Veenanath received treatment on his injured hand once he returned to the capital. Finding about the incident, Siddhartha rushed to check upon his king.

'My lord, your valour has protected the villagers. Your selfless dedication for our protection and well-being fills our hearts with gratitude,' eulogized the minister with sincerity.

'Siddhartha, that big cat was ferocious. It caught me off guard and I fell on my sword losing this thumb. You should have seen how I fought back and led it to the trap I had set,' said the excited king, while looking at the scribe who was documenting the jungle adventure.

'Dear Maharaj, you are utilizing God's gifts of intelligence and courage in praiseworthy public service,' said Siddhartha.

Mirthless at the proposal of sharing credit with God, the king gave the minister a blank look.

'Maharaj, the trap you had set for the leopard was brilliantly executed. Your fighting the leopard with an injured hand and your sharp presence of mind are all the grace of the Lord,' said the minister while reviewing the scribe's notes on how the king had set up the ditch trap.

'And what about the lost thumb? Is that too a gift of God?' asked the king, irritably.

'I beg your pardon, my lord, but yes, everything is the grace of the Supreme Lord,' said the minister with humility.

'Never mind, Siddhartha. What is the update on the revenue collection?' asked King Veenanath, changing the subject.

Later that day, taking advantage of the moment, Mihar Rajapathu, the state treasurer who envied Siddhartha, approached the king with a conspiratorial plan.

'Glory to the protector of the people! Maharaj, if you allow it, may I share with you an observation that I feel is in the best interest of your highness and our state?' he requested before bowing in respect while inspecting the king's face for any unfavourable expressions.

'Go on,' replied the king.

'Maharaj, I have observed that Prime Minister Siddhartha's attitude is not very loyal. How could he deal with your injury with such neglect? You had put your life at stake and fought a leopard with blood-gushing injured hands, losing a thumb!'

'Hmm . . . I felt awkward too at Siddhartha's reaction to this situation,' interjected the king.

'How could I sleep peacefully when I saw my own prime minister underplaying my king's sacrifice? Maharaj, I don't think he is taking your protection very seriously,' said the minister with a malicious heart.

'What do you reckon could be the reason behind this attitude, Mihar?' asked the king.

'I can't say. But one thing is for sure, he is trying to paint a picture of normality by equating everything as God's grace. Is he preparing a public opinion to accept everything as "God's grace" or is he cooking up something worse? Conspiracy or no conspiracy, I have heard many of your sincere followers concerned about Siddhartha's attitude. I don't think I have any reason to reprimand them when they doubt the prime minister's intentions,' concluded Mihar, successfully planting seeds of doubt about the prime minister in the king's heart.

Brooding over Mihar's ill constructs and afflicted by his injured hand, the king had a sleepless night. The doubts planted in his heart were watered by his own dislike of the minister.

'Siddhartha has never given me full credit for my work and hides his envy of me behind hollow praises of God,' he thought.

The next morning, the king passed an order to arrest Siddhartha and appointed Mihar as the new prime minister.

Many weeks later, the king and his newly appointed prime minister were on another forest excursion looking for some musk deer. In the chase, they were both captured by a group of forest-dwelling indigenous people who lived in the deep woodlands. The tribals carried their blindfolded royal captives deeper into the forest.

'Every ten years, we make a human sacrifice to the Big Belly Tree. This human is big and stout, we will offer him and this other smaller fellow can be let go after the ritual is over,' declared the tribal chief.

As the jungle natives began the preparation for their rituals, the tied king was inspected by the head priest.

'Stop!' exclaimed the tribal chief. 'This man cannot be offered in sacrifice. His body is not complete and will bring us bad luck,' said the priest pointing to the thumb-less left hand of the king who was tied upside down.

Turning his attention to their other captive, the priest decided that he was able-bodied and fit for the sacrifice. After sacrificing the new minister, one hunter among the tribals blindfolded the king and led his horse behind his own, out of the thick forest.

Reaching the border of the thicket, the tribal stopped and removed the king's blindfold.

Bidding the king goodbye, the tribal said, 'We have centuries-old jungle traditions; we treat the jungle as a wild person, living, breathing and providing for everyone. We offer it human meat once every ten years as compensation for taking everything from it. I am sorry you lost your friend, but that part of the jungle has belonged to our tribe for centuries and we follow our traditions there.'

Back at the palace, a disoriented king ordered the immediate release of his previous prime minister.

'I am sorry, Siddhartha! I realized today the import of what you always said. Yes, whatever happens is the grace of the Lord,' said the king, looking at his thumb-less hand with apologetic eyes. The minister smiled with a peaceful face. 'But while I escaped death, you were dishonoured and jailed without any fault. And that innocent Mihar got killed. How do I understand this to be God's grace?' asked the king.

'Maharaj, I understand that Mihar had poisoned your ears against me. Thanks to him, I was jailed or it would have been me in place of him, sacrificed. So it was all God's grace on me. Even Mihar was favoured by God to be killed by the tribals.'

'How?' asked the king.

Siddhartha explained: 'My spies informed me that he was in contact with our rivals. He was ambitious and was planning to dethrone you with their help. I was waiting for your return to raise a red flag with you. Mihar would have certainly been killed by you then.

'If he were to be successful with his plans, even then our army chief would have killed him. In any case, he was going to die, even at the hands of that rival king who treated him like a useful fool. His evil heart would have become the reason for the death of many innocent people as war ravaged our lands. His life being taken by the tribal people saved him from the bad karma of shedding innocent blood and treachery to the state.

'Everything is indeed God's grace on us,' concluded the wise minister.

> *mām upetya punar janma*
> *duḥkhālayam aśāśvatam*
> *nāpnuvanti mahātmānaḥ*
> *saṁsiddhiṁ paramāṁ gatāḥ*

This famous verse from the Gita points out the fundamental nature and objective reality of the world in honest, unsentimental terms.

Who can be naive enough to overlook the unrelenting assaults of nature's forces on us? Vedic observers point out three kinds of sufferings we all have to endure living in this world of matter. *Adhi-daivik-kalesh* are natural disturbances like earthquakes, heatwaves, floods, droughts, tsunamis, etc. *Adhi-bhutika-kalesh* are problems faced at the hands of other people like your boss, bad neighbours, relatives, back-stabbing friends, thieves, terrorists, mosquitoes, etc. *Adhi-aatmika-kalesh* is the suffering caused to us by our own bodies and minds like medical illnesses, allergies, weak eyesight, back pain, depression, etc.

PESSIMISTIC WORLDVIEW?

This world is a place of suffering (*dukhalayam*). Everyone we know, including ourselves, is going to die and everything we hold dear is going to get stale, grow old, become lost, get broken or left behind. Separation and suffering are the existential truths of living in the material world. All the spiritual traditions of the world understand these basic truths and have a positive objective in pointing them out to us. However, this declaration that the world is a place of misery is deemed as pessimistic by some. Nevertheless, the undeniable fact of this world as a distressful place serves as a healthy dose of reality to those seeking to find substantial happiness.

FIGHT OR FLIGHT? NO, TRANSCEND!

Life is neither as rosy as our daydreams nor as scary as our nightmares. Wisdom texts like the Gita impart a realistic vision and a level-headed approach to life. Through realizing our personal spiritual nature, we can handle our life's intricacies in a holistic manner without being driven by our fears or fantasies. Both fear and fantasy are connected with the preservation and pleasure of our body and mind. The Gita grounds us beyond these physical and psychological levels of our existence in our core indestructible spiritual nature.

The material world is often compared to a bottomless ocean of suffering where we are constantly tossed up and engulfed by high tides of persistent frustration and recurring unhappiness. While in the ocean, we cannot avoid getting shaken by the waves. Similarly, misery is completely unavoidable in this world. For that reason, yoga texts give us ways to responsibly deal with life's challenges and, at the same time, transcend our suffering altogether. Through time-tested paths like bhakti-yoga, which put us in direct union with the

Supreme Divine Lord, we can joyfully live a meaningful life despite the world being a place of suffering.

Our own bodies fail us from time to time; our minds either give up too quickly or stubbornly stick to damaging habits; our family and friends may not be able to help us beyond a certain capacity. When life feels like it's dark, the sun of yoga wisdom can enlighten us and help us transcend the suffering of the material world.

TWENTY-SEVEN

Conquering Pride

Human Quality: Humility

Lochan was not always a homeless man. He had lost his home and land in a village near Bhopal. Falling prey to greed, Lochan had invested heavily in a Ponzi scheme that a friend had introduced to him. The friend had made a great profit by investing a small amount and was now being paid by the company to earn even higher interest by bringing more investors to their 'investment bank'. Having seen his friend's new-found opulence, Lochan eagerly deposited his savings and very quickly started earning very high interest himself. Wanting to quadruple his earnings, Lochan started recruiting members on behalf of the company. However, this was all a hoax.

A few months later, the fraudsters, along with Lochan's 'friend', eloped with everyone's money. They vacated their grand rented offices overnight and fled. Lochan was met with an uproar from the group that he had recruited into the scheme. He pleaded with them that he was also a victim of the scheme, but this could not win their sympathies. To save himself, Lochan had to sell off his assets and settle the accounts.

Stamped a cheat, no one wanted to have a relationship with Lochan and he could not be hired for work in his village. Driven out of his hometown, a desperate Lochan moved to Kashi to start a new life. Suffering severe depression and unable to make sense of how quickly life had turned against him, Lochan became inactive and eventually fell into poverty. Sometimes eating at the local temples, Lochan otherwise lived by begging from pilgrims.

Once, Lochan went to a house and begged for some money. 'This poor beggar hasn't eaten a morsel in five days, is the lady of the house kind enough to give this unfortunate grandpa some money?' Lochan called out in his unique high-pitched begging voice, which sounded like a sobbing man singing. A young lady dressed in a nice silk saree came out and told Lochan to get lost.

'O daughter, God has given you so much and will give you more. I am asking only for a few coins,' petitioned Lochan in his sing-a-sob voice.

'Who is it, Suchitra?' somebody else called from inside.

'Nobody,' responded Suchitra.

The lady of the house came out and saw the beggar.

'Stay there baba, I will bring you some food and see if I can find an old kurta shirt for you,' said the young lady.

'Yes, give away everything, Meghana! Your parents married you off to my brother so you can turn us into beggars like this man,' taunted Suchitra.

'Don't you dare say a word about my parents. Your parents married you to that loafer Munish, now you spend half the month here. Go back to your in-laws!' came the response while Meghana went inside.

Unsure of how he should act, a hopeful Lochan sat down outside the house with his back to the door. A bitter catfight ensued and Lochan eavesdropped to see if Meghana was winning or losing. To his delight, Meghana said something very offensive to Suchitra who immediately ran out of the house.

'I will not return to this house until my brother does not personally bring you to apologize to me,' she said, standing at the door.

'What are you still doing here? Did you not hear me telling you to get lost?' Suchitra said, venting out all her frustration at Lochan, who had stationed himself next to the door.

'Ok, don't yell at me. I'm leaving. I'm old now and quickly get headaches,' said a hopeless Lochan as he picked himself up.

'Don't you dare go anywhere! Sit down, I am bringing you some food, some clothes and an old pair of shoes. You are not leaving without taking these things from me. I decide things here, not outsiders,' commanded Meghana while looking at her sobbing sister-in-law's face.

As Suchitra departed, Lochan's hopes revived. Delighted to be getting more than he had thought, Lochan started feeling excited.

'The boys back at the begging shores of the Ganga will have such a laugh. I will top everyone's story tonight,' Lochan giggled to himself as he waited for Meghana to return.

Just then another young girl, hardly a teenager, came from inside the house. Wearing salwar-kameez and a matching drape around her head, she spoke to the beggar in a sharp tone.

'My elder sister left the home crying because of you. Get lost now and never come back here,' she said. Realizing that he had become the cause of a family feud, Lochan got up and left without a word.

Crossing the road and walking just a little distance, Lochan begged from another lady who had stepped out of a nearby temple. While the lady looked for some change in her purse, Lochan started narrating his experience.

'Just see how kind you are sister, helping a poor old man like me. That young lady in that house over there was extremely rude to me. She told me to get lost when I asked for one roti,' said Lochan.

Realizing that Lochan was pointing towards her house, the elderly lady asked him to confirm which house he was talking about. Now that it was confirmed he had been sent away from her house, the lady asked Lochan to come with her.

Having reached her house door, the old lady commanded, 'Meghana, come out right now!'

'Coming Mummy ji,' came the response.

'How dare you send away this poor old beggar without giving him anything? Just look at his poor face. Lord! Have I married my son to a heartless person? Do you have no kindness left in you?' questioned the elderly lady.

Just then, the teenage girl who had sent Lochan away came out and told her mother what had happened.

'Mother, Meghana bhabhi made Suchitra didi cry when she tried to stop bhabhi from giving away something to this old man and then she left and she said she will not come here till bhaiya brings bhabhi to apologize to didi,' said the young girl all in one breath.

Fuming in anger, the mother-in-law now correctly understood what had happened. She realized that she had wrongly assumed that her daughter-in-law had turned the beggar away when it was her daughter who had done so.

'Suchitra stopped Meghana from giving charity to this beggar?' said the mother-in-law in shock.

'Yes, Mummy ji, I tried to . . .'

Interjecting, the mother-in-law said, 'Enough of this!'

Seeing the temperament of the mother-in-law, Lochan's heart finally felt relieved.

In an unapologetic tone, the mother-in-law turned towards Lochan.

'Get lost, you are not getting anything.'

Confused, Lochan said, 'But it was you only who brought me over . . .'

Interjecting, the mother-in-law declared, 'It is my house. My daughter-in-law cannot decide what you will get. Nor do my daughters carry the privilege of throwing you out. This is a privilege limited to me alone. I am the boss here and I now want you to get lost!'

> *tri-vidham narakasyedam*
> *dvāram nāśanam ātmanaḥ*
> *kāmaḥ krodhas tathā lobhas*
> *tasmād etat trayam tyajet*

Friends, this wisdom nugget from the Gita points out to human society the three gateways leading to a hellish life. Every sane person is advised here to give up lust, anger and greed, the pathways to hellish self-destruction. (Bhagavad Gita 16.21)

ON LUST

Spiritual traditions proclaim that lust is our greatest enemy. Lust epitomizes selfishness by dehumanizing people and reducing them to mere objects for our sensual gratification. It torments us like a maniac master, unrelenting in its demands and unforgiving in its presence. Once triggered, lust constantly provokes us, numbing our sense of discretion and rewarding us with short-term pleasure. But in due course, lust robs us of all our inner peace and joy. But how is lust to be defeated?

ON ANGER

The fire of anger ignites quickly and leaves behind ruins of burned objects, relationships and hearts. Anger's illusive power deceives us often with its false justification to express it out. Sabotaging our intelligence, anger leaves no room for considering the long-term consequences of our outbursts. Rage blinds us and we wilfully jump off the safe bridge of our calm intelligence meant to carry us from problems to solutions, into a raging river of violent impulses. Often, the satisfaction achieved through an angry outburst against our wrongdoers is too dear to give away even if it is damaging for us. How is anger to be conquered?

ON GREED

It is not bad to be ambitious. Ambitions can bring us a sense of direction, focus, dedication, purpose, energy and excitement. But often, promising ambitions turn dark when tainted with greed. Touched by the poison of greed for personal gain, ambition can turn deadly. Always wanting and expecting more, greed dries away all our satisfaction. The feeling of never having enough develops into a chronic itch that does not rest even when it bleeds on scratching. Enslaved by greed, the loyal turn treacherous, the faithful turn murderous and protectors turn tyrants. How is greed to be pacified?

THE YOGA PERSPECTIVE

The Gita explains that in our essence, we all are pleasure-seeking spiritual beings. Ignorant of our own spirituality, we experiment through the medium of our bodies and minds to try and attain unending happiness.

Unfortunately, there are two problems with this plan. Firstly, our senses and mental faculties are limited; even if we have an abundant amount of things, we do not have the sensual power to enjoy them. Secondly (and more fundamentally), due to the incompatibility between the happiness drawn from material means and our spiritual needs, that at our core we are pleasure-seeking, material happiness becomes the cause of frustration and lack of fulfilment. Material happiness is diametrically opposite.

The vices of lust, anger and greed are closely related to this lack of fulfilment deep within us. Such insatiability and dissatisfaction bring trouble because they trigger us to want more and ignorantly keep us busy searching for a lasting satisfaction that does not exist.

Thus, negation, repression and gratification prove equally insufficient to win over the prodding of these inner enemies.

THE YOGA SOLUTION

To win over these dark forces, we need to cultivate inner strength through spiritual development. Time-tested spiritual practices such as yoga and meditation lift us above our physical impulses and mental instincts. Situated in our pure non-material essence, we experience inner joy that is hard to find externally through the possession of objects and experience of sensuality. Such spiritual growth empowers us to resist temporary materialistic drives.

Furthermore, we can find solace in our inner being by strengthening our intelligence. Having an understanding of spiritual knowledge and practising spirituality honestly gives us the intelligence to control the mind and senses.

We saw how Lochan's greed ruined his life and anger spoiled the peace of the ladies' household. To rise above such petty weaknesses of the heart, we need to infuse our life with meaning and worthy purpose, above and beyond what the world of false promises can offer. In wisdom traditions, such meaning and purpose is found internally. Reviving our connection with the Supreme Lord, who resides in everyone's heart as the supreme witness, guide and friend, is the true means for cultivating inner strength, finding real happiness and lasting fulfilment.

TWENTY-EIGHT

Thirst Dilemma

Human Quality: Giving

Outside his college life, Preetam was a treasure hunter. His dare-devil antics had won him small fortunes, but had also put his life at risk many times. Since childhood he had heard about the lost treasures in the Thar Desert of Jaisalmer. The Thar had an open invitation to one and all. There was a huge chest of jewels waiting to be found. Many, over the years, had attempted to find this treasure, but had lost their lives with only their bones found by others.

Buried somewhere under those beautiful sand dunes was a treasure chest that belonged to a bygone Rajput queen. Folklore had it that the jewels were to be found by the king of that queen, reborn centuries later as a tall, fair and handsome prince from the mountains. It was believed that once the treasure was found, the royal couple would reunite in their present incarnations, with the queen being a famous dancer.

Preetam ticked the description . . . well almost. He was tall, fair, handsome and the son of a schoolteacher in Shimla. He was also affectionately called Prince by his family and friends. This term of endearment was no mere coincidence;

it was, according to Preetam, a literal description of him—'a prince from the mountains!'

As far as Preetam was concerned, the prophecy of the treasure chest would come true through him. That treasure box contained not only an incredible wealth of jewels, but also the key to his soulmate's heart. Preetam spent many a night dreaming about the treasure and guessing who his queen could be. Was it a Bollywood star? Was it a girl who lived among the Hollywood hills? Or was it a French ballerina who performed in theatre?

It was time for action. For a long time, Preetam 'Prince' Kaul had heard, dreamt and read about the treasure folklore. Onwards to Jaisalmer with supplies to support him for two weeks, Preetam had set into his life's greatest adventure. Having studied electromagnetism at college, he had built a makeshift handheld metal detector before starting from Shimla. Wrapping a coil of copper wire around an iron horseshoe and then hooking up his gizmo to a battery, Preetam was ready for the job at hand. With James Maxwell's equations in his mind, a compass and his unfailing intuition, Preetam arrived in Jaisalmer.

Time was passing quickly. It was Preetam's seventh night of searching now. The sun beat down in the daytime so Preetam decided to do most of his searching in the cooler night. But the romantic feelings of becoming the rich husband of a dancing beauty overnight were fast evaporating under the Thar heat. 'Bleep! Bleep! Bleep!' the metal detector's sound of excitement was slowly turning into a call for frustration. The treasure found so far consisted of a couple of empty cola cans, nails and a builder's hammer.

But our 'prince from the mountains' had determination. He had dived to the Sutlej's riverbed and found many sunken smartphones, GoPros and coins of various denominations and nationalities. Tonight had not been very promising so far, but his intuition had convinced him to extend his search past the cooler part of the early morning. But soon enough, away from his camping spot and now stranded, Preetam realized his big mistake to expose his intentions to the afternoon sun.

Exhausted and extremely thirsty, Preetam was now crawling around, dehydrated. He knew that if he fainted before he found water, it could turn out to be fatal. Thankfully, he saw a hut and as he walked inside, to his great ecstasy, there was a water hand pump in the corner. With great hope, Preetam started working on the handle of the hand pump. Apart from a reconfirming gurgling sound, no water came out. In spite of his best efforts, water would not come out, but continued to sing underground.

Suddenly his eyes fell on a worn-out styrofoam box. Inside, there was a sealed water bottle.

'Ah! Water, the elixir of life,' exclaimed Preetam with the bottle shining in his hands.

As his hands opened the lid, his eyes read the note stuck on the face of the bottle.

'1. Pour this water at the bottom of the hand pump. Then work the pump handle. Water will come out of the tap.

'2. Make sure that you refill this bottle and keep it back the way it was.

'3. Reconsider what you really value in life.'

Indecisive, a dehydrated Preetam looked at the water in the bottle in his hand and the old water hand pump in the corner.

'I am too tired and fear the worst. I need this water. God helps those who help themselves! Should I drink the water and save my life, or should I risk pouring it and hope that the hand pump works? What if the water doesn't come out? I will die of thirst having poured away the only water available. A bird in hand is worth two in the bush,' thought Preetam.

'But what about someone else who will be in my position in the future? "No one has ever become poor by giving", "Help yourself by helping others," "We only have what we give, beta,"' Preetam remembered his mother reading these famous quotes to him when he was a child.

'O All-Knowing Supreme Lord of the Universe, I am in a dire situation. I am a soul surrendered unto You, now please guide me from within as to what I must do,' Preetam prayed sincerely as he sat down on the floor with tears sliding out of his eyes.

A few minutes of meditative silence later, free from a screaming-fearful mind and a hankering-calculative intelligence, Preetam stood up again.

'I'll follow the instructions on the bottle.'

With reverence and faith, Preetam poured the water of the bottle at the bottom of the hand pump. As his twitchy hands started moving the handle of the pump again, precious beads of anticipative sweat decorated his forehead. With the same old gurgling sound, Preetam's act of faith was being tested. The sound continued for a few minutes and then grew louder and within moments, water came gushing out.

Preetam looked at the roof of the hut, acknowledging God first and then drank plenty of water to his satisfaction.

Then he filled the bottle as before, put the airtight seal on it and with his map marker, made an entry on the bottle sticker.

'4. God has proven to me that these steps work. Have faith and follow these instructions if you need water from this pump.'

Signed, 'A happily single and poor prince from the mountains.'

> *udyama sāhasa dhairyaṁ*
> *buddhiḥ śaktiḥ parākramaḥ*
> *ṣaḍete yatra vartante*
> *tatra devaḥ sahāyakṛta*
> *(Subhāṣīta ratnākar(sphuta))*

Friends, this nice verse presents the recipe for success in life. To achieve success, one needs *diligent and continuous efforts* to achieve one's objective, *courage* to deal with the challenges on the way, *patience* for the efforts to bear fruit, *intelligence* to make the right adjustments as required, *power* to stand against opposition and failures, and *boldness* to deal with the unknown. It is said here that one who works like this attracts even God Almighty's assistance.

Yoga philosophy promotes the idea that human life is meant for giving and sharing. Charity and sacrifice for helping others in fact helps the receiver and the giver. The receiver feels valued as a cherished member of God's universal family. At the same time, when done in the spirit of serving others, givers expand their consciousness by attuning to concerns beyond their self-interest.

WHAT IS CHARITY AND WHAT IS SACRIFICE?

Charity is a physical expression of compassion and sacrifice. Generally, charity is extended to those in a position lower than ours and a sacrifice is made for those superior to us.

We do not give charity to our parents, teachers, our superiors or to a house of God. For them, we make a sacrifice of what can be used for our own comfort in their service. Thus, a sacrifice is best made as an act of gratitude.

Similarly, while charity is offered to those in a more vulnerable position than ours, it does not mean that the receiver is an inferior person to us.

In the Gita, the act of giving has been analysed both at the level of external action and internal intention.

THE GIVER'S CONSCIOUSNESS DECIDES THE GIFT'S VALUE

Andrew Carnegie, one of the richest Americans in history, famously said, 'It is more difficult to give money away intelligently than to earn it in the first place.' Wilfully sharing what we have with a deserving candidate, at an appropriate time without expectation of return and with a good heart, is an act of giving done right. Such acts are performed in *sattva-guna*, or in a mode of goodness. A useful and non-violent gift offered to a respected senior with a thankful heart is beneficial for both the receiver and the giver. It brings a deep sense of fulfilment and ingrains selflessness in the giver's heart and harnesses feelings of affection in the receiver's heart.

A contribution made for the sake of broadcasting our own financial status, for public recognition or for some future reward in mind, is done in *rajo-guna* or an act in a mode of passion. Such giving is more self-serving, despite the external act of benefiting others. Boosting one's own ego, it lacks the benevolent potency that can have a sublime effect in purifying our heart from self-centredness. When giving becomes a public relations tool or is done for social status, the giver doesn't truly benefit from it.

Finally, charity and sacrifice can be made in *tamo-guna* or an act of giving performed in a mode of darkness. It includes giving to an undeserving person, at an inappropriate time, for the wrong reasons, or when giving is done indifferently in a careless mood or in a disrespectful way. Such giving does harm both to the giver and to the receiver. Giving money to a drug addict without considering his plight or the danger he may pose to others around is a gross mistake. Such thoughtless giving is unenlightened and bears negative fruits.

THE HIGHEST GIFT TO GIVE AND TO RECEIVE

Friends, wisdom texts like the Gita help us clarify our reasons and purify our motivations while giving. Yoga texts explain that, as spiritual souls at our core, our needs are essentially spiritual in nature. Material means to find fulfilment for our deeper needs (like love and care) will always fail.

The Supreme Lord, God or Krishna, is the supreme whole of whom we are infinitesimal parts. Fulfilment and perfection of the part is only found in connection with the whole. Like Preetam, as spiritual souls, we all are lost in the desert of material existence. While on our treasure hunt for happiness, we may find many empty cans of material possessions or shining nails of sensual pleasure, but such things simply distract and bind us to temporary happiness.

We are best found when spiritual teachers come and provide us maps to escape the desert. Through the spiritual knowledge of the soul and its relationship with the Supreme Soul, we can reorient ourselves in this vast desert of material existence. By following their directions, we can come to the shelter of the house of bhakti-yoga where a fountain of spiritual happiness flows limitlessly. By thus rising from material consciousness to spiritual consciousness, we come out of the desert to the oasis—the spiritual world where life is eternal and ecstatic.

TWENTY-NINE

Palace or Guest House

Human Quality: Detachment

Akinchan Krishna Swami was travelling through the kingdom of King Sushant Singh Dogra in Jammu. He had heard that the king had become morally wayward and had grown attached to women and wine. Feeling compassion for the citizens of Jammu, the monk decided to help teach the king the path to responsible behaviour.

One night, the swami went to see the king at the palace, but the guards turned him away from the door, 'The king has instructed us not to allow any holy men inside. He says he is not interested in seeing any beggars.'

Understanding the situation, the swami used the sword of words to get the king's attention.

'I am not here to beg; I have come here to give. It is late now and I was wondering if I could stay here in this big guest house for tonight,' said the swami.

'Which guest house?' asked the guard.

'This big cottage you are guarding,' replied the swami.

'Are you mad, old man? This is not a big cottage, this is the royal palace of King Sushant Singh Dogra!' said the irritated guard.

'Don't be a fool. You are mistaken. Go ask your king if I can get a room in this hostel for tonight,' commanded the sage.

Irritated and wanting to teach him a lesson, the guard went in and informed the king about a beggar monk calling the gorgeous royal palace a guest house.

'Bring him here! I will fix his vision. How dare he insult the royal legacy of the Dogras?' said the king angrily when informed about the monk's insistence.

Once inside, the monk was presented before the king.

'My guards are telling me that you are insulting our royal prestige. Does this palace look like a boarding house to you?' asked the king.

'Yes, very precisely so,' said the monk peacefully.

'Hmm, I am sure you have stayed at different public rest-houses or government shelter homes. Do these massive rooms with silken curtains, ivory vases and precious chandeliers look familiar to you?' poked the king, intending insult.

'O king, who stayed here before you occupied it?' asked the monk.

Pointing to a large portrait behind his throne, the king said loudly, 'His Royal Majesty King Prashant Singh Dogra, my respected father.'

'And before Maharaja Prashant Singh, who was staying here?' asked the monk further.

'His Royal Highness King Nishant Singh Dogra, my revered grandfather,' replied the king, pointing to another huge painting of a bygone monarch.

'And before Maharaja Nishant Singh, who was staying here?' asked the monk further.

Pointing to yet another huge vintage portrait, this time of his great-grandfather, the king said with pride, 'The glory of the Dogra lions, His Excellency King Dishant Singh Dogra.'

'Well, where are King Prashant Singh, Maharaja Nishant Singh and Sahib Dishant Singh now?' asked the monk, looking straight into the king's eyes.

'What do you mean!' yelled King Sushant Singh.

'Dear child, they have all moved onwards. They stayed in this palatial building for a few years, enjoyed the hospitality and fought wars to pay their dues for the bed and breakfast. Then, with the announcement of time, they had to leave everything behind. We are all travellers and we continue our journey in this world until we work our way back home, back to Godhead. But does your forefathers' stay in this palace not sound like a travellers' stay at any other guest house to you?' asked the humble sage with a serene expression.

The king fell silent as he contemplated the deep import of the swami's words.

'Son, we are all travellers. Even within the guest house of our own bodies, we are to stay for some time, enjoy the facilities like eating, drinking and being merry. We pay our dues by working, feeding and sleeping. We stay in this body's guest house for a limited period and have to depart when the sun of time sets on us. Then, we are born again, to occupy another bodily guest house. And like this, we are all travellers until we find our way back home, back to Godhead.'

Realizing the transient nature of the ephemeral world, the king said to the monk, 'Thank you for enlightening me. While in the guest house of the body, how should we live?'

The monk replied with gravity, 'While here, like me, you should endeavour to only eat nectar, only sleep on a bed of flowers, always be guarded in an iron fort and simply enjoy the company of a beautiful woman.'

Bewildered by these words coming from a celibate monk, the king asked for an explanation.

Explaining, Akinchan Krishna Swami said, 'Only eat nectar! This means eat only when you are hungry. This way, your food will be digested well and keep you disease-free. Hunger is the best sauce as they say. As explained in the seventeenth chapter of the Gita, when food is eaten in moderation, it is digested well and is as good as nectar.'

Clarifying further, the monk said, 'Sleeping on a bed of flowers means to sleep when you are actually tired. Work hard during the day for the upkeep of your body, and well-being of your family and society. Then when you are tired, you get a deep and sound sleep. So, when you have earned your sleep like this, then wherever you lie down, it feels like a bed of flowers. You are sure to get refreshing sleep after a hard day's work, not otherwise.'

'What is the iron fort you mentioned?' asked the king.

'Always live in the association of the noble-hearted devotees of the Lord. In the iron fort of their guidance, you will be protected from the temptations and passing allurements of this world. There, inside that fort of saintly association, you can easily subdue even your inner enemies like lust, anger, greed, pride, illusion and envy.'

'And what about the company of a beautiful woman that you mentioned?' asked the king.

Concluding the purport to his final instruction the sage explained, 'The company of *Vidya-vadhu*, or the bride of wisdom is the most enjoyable. Vidya or knowledge has to be married; this means one has to develop a personal relationship with spiritual wisdom. By studying under learned teachers and by then putting into practice the philosophy they teach, you can develop such a relationship. This life partner will serve you throughout your life, guide you and support you through thick and thin, like a faithful wife.'

> *yoga-yukto viśuddhātmā*
> *vijitātmā jitendriyaḥ*
> *sarva-bhūtātma-bhūtātmā*
> *kurvann api na lipyate*

Friends, this verse from the Gita (Bhagavad Gita 5.7) gives us the key to freedom even while we take on the responsibilities of life. Every action creates a reaction. Work performed without spiritual understanding creates karma or bondage to the results of our work, both good and bad. However, work undertaken in spiritual wisdom frees us from the dualities of good and bad, and reactions born of desiring and detesting.

Through Vedic philosophy, we come to understand that everything and everyone has their origin in the supreme cause of all causes, the Supreme Lord. Enlightened work brings that philosophical truth to the forefront when we act.

One becomes happy and completely liberated from the bondage of karma, which is inherent in all worldly deeds, simply by undertaking one's work in spiritual consciousness of the Supreme. Working thus, one becomes a master of one's own mind and senses and dear to everyone. An enlightened soul, though always working, is never entangled in the worldly mesh of karma. In comparison, an attached worker lives a miserable, self-centred life driven by aversions and attractions like King Sushant Singh Dogra before he met Akinchan Krishna Swami.

PLANS, PROBLEMS AND ATTACHMENTS

Since the soul is an active pleasure-seeking entity by nature, life's fulfilment is achieved through gaining lasting happiness. We expect to achieve that happiness as we work to build our life, our career and our dreams. We expect that we will tweak things when we encounter problems beyond the scope of our planning. Most people end up in trouble as they try to alter their plans to address or eliminate the problems.

Identifying and being heavily attached to our plans makes us myopic. Focusing too much on our goals distracts us from executing our plans well. We begin to sink if we cling too rigidly to our plans or get too affected by the prospect of losing our goals. Resilience is required, but stubbornness born of attachments is unhealthy. Often, we don't realize it, but a lot of our suffering is caused by our attachment to self-defeating habits or similar unhelpful thinking patterns. Yoga texts therefore emphasize the place of detachment in life.

WHAT IS DETACHMENT?

Vedic wisdom explains that detachment means becoming indifferent to the mind's schemes for material enjoyment.

Such indifference is not artificially or prematurely enforced. It grows organically in us.

Lifelong promises of pleasure and fulfilment offered by material things and relationships create a hollowness throughout our lives. We end up feeling, 'Is this it?' as we achieve our material goals. We can use such unfulfilling experiences as the launchpad to explore the spiritual dimension as laid down by authentic wisdom texts like the Gita. We stand to gain a higher form of spiritual happiness through the Gita's process of bhakti-yoga. With our hearts contented with higher spiritual happiness, detachment from all forms of lower material pleasure and lamentation from the resultant frustration naturally arises.

Broadening our vision from the material to the spiritual is the first step to detachment. As a side benefit, when detachment grows within us, it gives us an objective perception of reality, unaltered by emotions born of attraction or aversion. It makes our heart soft with self-love and compassion for others, seeing the always-failing struggle of the mind and the senses for the sake of lasting happiness. In the absence of the higher spiritual happiness, dry renunciation can turn people hard-hearted. Those who despise the world as a place of false attachments and suffering take up such unhealthy and fruitless renunciation.

Friends, when our plans begin to interfere with our inner spiritual development, it is time to let them go. However, we should not do so haphazardly or for escaping responsibility. Detachment enables us to productively use our power of discernment. Without being misled by the prospects of enjoyment or fears of failure, discernment made available through detachment can guide us to make the right choices.

DETACHMENT—PROTECTOR AND GUIDE

A baby monkey is unwilling to let go of the food placed in a pot with a small opening. All it has to do is open its fist, let go of the food, slide its hand out and run away to safety. But it sticks to its plan, remains unwilling to let go of the sweet-smelling food and is easily captured by the hunter. Even if our plans fructify, it can often become an obstacle to our real happiness. Throughout our life, we may need to let go of what we have, to allow us the opportunity to venture into a world of new possibilities.

We can't grow in life if we are too attached to how we wish or envision it to be. As our plans or lack of planning unfold outcomes that we dislike, it is time to let go and start afresh. In the absence of wise detachment, we either end up hating and blaming ourselves or others due to the bitterness of not having fulfilled our desires.

DETACHMENT THROUGH ATTACHMENT

Some people misunderstand detachment to be hard-hearted indifference, apathetic action or total abandonment of the world. Such 'detachment' is troublesome and unsustainable. While theoretical meditation on the spiritual may bring us some momentary inner calm and a feeling of relief, it is insufficient to cater to the soul's everlasting need for joy and fulfilment. These higher gifts are only available in connection with our supreme well-wishing friend, the perfect reciprocator, the Supreme Lord.

Real satisfaction comes only by the fulfilment of our spiritual needs. And our deepest need is for love. That love finds its culmination in the reservoir of all satisfaction, the Supreme Lord or Krishna. Therefore, if we want to detach ourselves from the material conception of life, we must begin to attach ourselves to the spiritual understanding that sits in our relationship with Krishna himself.

THIRTY

The Coconut Story

Human Quality: Wisdom

Prince Mrugank Charu Varma was proclaimed by his father as the heir apparent of their vast kingdom located in the deep south Malabar Coast of India. Being exporters of aromatic spices, raw and dry coconut and jumbo-sized cashew kernels made the kingdom one of the most affluent of the time. The beauty of the kingdom attracted tourists from all over the country to its beaches, hill stations, backwaters and beautiful tropical forests.

Prince Mrugank received a great education and could fluently speak many languages. An expert in archery and swordsmanship, the prince was also respected for his knowledge of law and justice. From a young age, the prince showed a special interest in the arts. Skilled at playing the *mridangam* drums and the violin, the prince wrote much of the background music for his dance-drama shows.

Once, while the prince was on a reclusive trip to a hill forest, he ran into a monk. Attracted by the glow of the monk's face, the prince got off his horse and folded his hands in respect.

'Welcome, your attire tells me that you eat in a golden plate. How is your *swaasthya*?' the wise man asked.

Introducing himself, Mrugank responded that he was healthy and fit as a response to the swaasthya question.

'That's nice that you are healthy and fit, but are you swaasthya?' the monk continued to ask.

'Like I said, I'm healthy and fit. Is that not what the word swaasthya means? Or is there another meaning for it that you are applying and inquiring about, O sage?' the prince asked politely.

'The general meaning of swaasthya is health. But it is actually a compound word made of two parts, "Swa" which means "the self" and "Asthya" which means "positioned or situated in". So, my question is that, while you are healthy and fit, are you situated in the self or not?' explained the sage.

The intelligent prince understood that the monk was an enlightened man and that he had an opportunity to ask deeper questions to the sage.

Tying his horse to a nearby tree, Mrugank bowed to the sage and requested him for some answers.

'O sage, I am the heir apparent of this vast kingdom. I have all the riches in the world. I live a luxurious life of royal comforts. I have nothing to worry about or fear. I have access to all sorts of pleasures, the company of beautiful women and the support of powerful people. I have everything that most people in the world can only dream of. Yet, after all this, I find that my heart feels empty. Though I keep myself busy enjoying singing, dancing, hunting, dining and socializing, the lacking in my heart does not go away. What is the cause of this?' asked the prince with candid honesty.

'O prince, first consider this for a minute. The very body that you utilize for these exhilarating experiences you have mentioned is the greatest enemy of your happiness,' said the sage.

'My body is my enemy?' asked the prince with an unsure expression.

'Yes, from the perspective of the quality of happiness you seek, your body is your enemy. While you wish to engage the body endlessly in pleasure pursuits, the same body does not allow for those pleasure episodes to last long. It hits a saturation point rapidly. Since the body's capacity to enjoy is limited, the very body which is the means to what you seek as enjoyment becomes a barrier to that enjoyment. Not that you've had enough, but the body will not allow you to have more. Is it not so?' asked the sage, concluding his point.

The prince thought for a few moments and responded, 'But that's the case with everyone, since we are all made this way. Perhaps, that's as good as it gets. Happiness . . .'

Interjecting, the sage asked, 'Son, I cannot consider such happiness to be actual happiness. The happiness that fluctuates is not real happiness. Don't you see how the very objects that give you pleasure now become the source of boredom, frustration or hankering for more of the same later? Happiness that ends in misery is just another form of sorrow. Have you ever considered that your seeking endless happiness in life points to a different possibility both of what you think of yourself and of happiness itself?'

'Dear sage, I see your point. There definitely seems to be a disconnect somewhere between my constant desire for happiness and the depleting experience of happiness that I get through my body. I want to understand what the cause of this disconnect and dissatisfaction is,' said the intelligent prince.

'Son, it is the incompatibility between your core spiritual nature and the material means that you employ to fulfil your deeper spiritual needs. What we actually seek is spiritual happiness, but what we explore and settle for is material happiness. The incompatibility between the spiritual need and material means is the cause of this disconnect and the root of dissatisfaction of your heart,' answered the monk.

'Our spiritual nature? What is this core spiritual nature that you are talking about? I have always wondered, is there more to me than what I currently understand?' asked the prince further.

Pointing to a tall coconut tree nearby, the monk asked the prince to fetch him a coconut.

Taking off his royal turban and fancy shoes, the tall, dark and handsome prince climbed the tree, got a coconut and placed it in front of the monk.

Pointing to the coconut, the monk asked the prince, 'What is it?'

Unsure if it was a serious question and a little confused, the prince blurted, 'A coconut!'

'Peel it,' requested the monk.

Putting his dagger and big arms to use, the prince peeled off the fibrous husk-coir that covered the coconut, putting the waste aside.

Now pointing to the circular hard shell in his student's hands, the monk asked again, 'What is it?'

With a thoughtful expression and arched eyebrows, the prince replied, 'A coconut.'

'Open it,' said the monk.

With a strong hit of one of his metal bangles, the prince cracked open the shell.

Pointing to the white, soft coconut inside the shell, the monk asked again, 'What is it?'

Intrigued by the evolving question, the prince responded with a gentle smile, 'A Co. Co. Nut!'

Pointing now to all three—the husk, the cracked shell and the white, soft coconut, the monk asked, 'Which one of these is the coconut?'

Considering thoughtfully, the prince pointed out to the edible part.

'So, are you saying that the husk and the shell are not coconut?' asked the monk in an interrogative tone.

'Well, they are coconut, but not the coconut,' the prince said, laughing at his own answer.

'Elaborate,' said the sage.

'The real coconut hides underneath these other layers of the coconut,' came the reply.

'Exactly. This husk of the coconut is akin to our body, the external covering. The shell inside this physical body is the psychological body we have—the mind-intelligence-ego unit. But it is the fruit beyond the unseen psychological covering that is the real us—the soul. The body and the mind belong to us, but not the real us,' explained the learned guru.

'So, the soul is the real us and our core nature is spiritual. Therefore, material things are unable to give us lasting satisfaction and happiness. Now I get the incompatibility you spoke about earlier. How do we identify our spiritual nature? If we are essentially spiritual, then how does that spiritual nature manifest?' asked the prince.

'Simply by observation you can come to understand your axiomatic, natural and intrinsic spiritual nature. Think in terms of that which is common to all living beings and which is the existential feature of everyone. You can then safely conclude it as the core nature of the soul,' continued the sage.

'Yes, that was my question too. What is the inherent nature of the soul?' asked Mrugank humbly.

'Service. It is service that is this intrinsic nature of the soul. Either you serve your body, your plans, your family, community, society, nation, the world, or your religion. In every sphere of your activities, service is the common minimum denominator. To offer service is the essential function of the soul,' emphasized the monk.

The wise prince said, 'I serve my parents, my father serves the state, our subjects serve each other and collectively, we serve the nation. Our horses serve our military troops, who serve them in return. Even the cat serves its kittens. I think I understand your point, but how does knowing all this address my lack of fulfilment and dissatisfaction? How do I become completely happy? Simply by knowing that I am a spiritual being different from my mind and body?'

'Mrugank, for most people, the sphere of service revolves around themselves. Limited to the service of their bodily cravings and mental whims, people end up frustrated all too quickly. For others, the sphere of service includes others, to their extended selves in the form of their family, friends, clubs, nationality, etc. An increasing degree of fulfilment can be naturally achieved by extending our service tendency from ourselves to others in a selfless mood. The key to happiness is to move from selfishness to selflessness through loving service. But even these forms of service are essentially material and while they provide a deeper sense of fulfilment, they are insufficient to fully satisfy us. Complete fulfilment and real unending joy is exclusively available only by service to the spiritual source of everything and everyone, the Supreme Personality of Godhead,' concluded the monk.

> *ye hi samsparśa-jā bhogā*
> *duḥkha-yonaya eva te*
> *ādy-antavantaḥ kaunteya*
> *na teṣu ramate budhaḥ*
> (Bhagavad Gita 5.22)

Friends, this verse appears in the fifth chapter of the Gita. It appeals to our contemplative side, pointing out to us that happiness experienced through our sensual outlets eventually leads to misery.

While sensual temptations are laden with the promise of pleasure, such pleasure is short-lived and leaves us in a restless state of wanting more. The gap between our needs and our wants causes us dissatisfaction and frustration. Sensual happiness has a beginning and an end, but our need for happiness is permanent, so we cannot be satisfied with experiencing happiness only through the senses. Thus, sensual desires that titillate us initially, torment us eventually. Isn't this precisely what we have repeatedly experienced in our lives?

PLEASURE-SEEKING POINTING TO HIGHER POSSIBILITIES

'Life, liberty and the pursuit of happiness' is a well-known phrase in the United States Declaration of Independence.

It says that these three have been given to all humans by their creator, and which governments are created to protect.

Vedic wisdom explains that at our core we are spiritual souls, parts of the complete whole who is 'sac-cid-ānanda-vigrahaḥ', that is, the supreme person who is the divine embodiment of eternality, knowledge and bliss. Parts share the properties of the whole, thus we are persons who are ever seeking an eternal existence (sat), well-informed by knowledge (cid) and saturated with pleasure (ananda).

The American wise men had incorporated the right of life, liberty and the pursuit of happiness as 'unalienable rights' of the people. Vedic wisdom has additionally included knowledge as the guide for us to pursue these rights, identifying that indiscriminate sensuality leads to inevitable misery. Without proper knowledge, we are overwhelmed by an ocean of material temptations invoked in us by naked propaganda.

This revelation of the negative nature of sensual pleasure is only done to protect us from unnecessary suffering. The primary purpose of such wisdom is to help us experience the superlative nature of spiritual pleasure. Such wisdom sharpens our intelligence to help us see through the facade of sensual pleasure and its ever-alluring false promise of fulfilment. It helps us recognize the inadequacy of material pleasure and find superior spiritual bliss in our pursuit of happiness.

THIRTY-ONE

Provocations and Self-Control

Human Quality: Self-Control

Nandini was in the grocery store with her two kids.

'Mummy, I want strawberries,' said Haripriya.

'And I want ice cream. Didi can have one of the ice creams from the packet if she shares those strawberries with me,' said little Balaram.

As the mother went through the different aisles of fruits and vegetables getting her weekly stock, her well-mannered kids followed along patiently.

'Relax, Banita, it's ok!' said another mother in the store, looking at her little daughter who had started throwing temper tantrums. The mother held her daughter's hand gently as she browsed through her list of remaining items to buy.

'It's boring in here and I want to go now,' said the little girl as she grew impatient.

'Just a few more minutes, Banita, and we are leaving,' said the mother as she rushed to put a bag of tomatoes in her shopping basket.

A little while later, the girl screamed, 'I want to go! I want to go! I want to go!'

'That's all right, Banita. Take it easy,' said the mother, finalizing her shopping.

With anxious, concerned eyes, Haripriya and Balaram saw the little girl crying. Nandini looked at the mother of the child with sympathy. Collecting her final items from the refrigerated section of the shop, the mother proceeded to the checkout counter. The little girl threw herself on the floor, started kicking in the air and screamed at the top of her lungs.

'I want to go now!'

With a long breath out, the mother responded, 'Relax, Banita, we are out in two minutes. We are just paying now. It's almost over.'

Nandini paid for her items at another counter and rushed with her kids to catch up with the other mother and her daughter.

'You have so much patience. I am so impressed. I wish I could treat my kids with such composure and calmness the way you dealt with your daughter,' said Nandini to the other mother.

Turning to the little girl, Nandini said, 'Banita, your mummy really loves you . . .'

The mother then spoke to Nandini, 'Thanks for your kind words, but my daughter's name is Devyani and I am Banita.'

Surprised, Nandini looked at her co-shopper with a confused smile on her face.

'Whenever Devyani throws temper tantrums, I remind myself to remain calm. She is too little to be held responsible. She doesn't even understand what she is doing. So, as the adult, it is my responsibility to not lose patience and become provoked by her innocent flare-ups,' said Banita, looking affectionately at little Devyani.

'Wow, that's amazing motherhood!' said an appreciative Nandini.

'Do you have ten minutes, can we talk? Can I get us some fresh juice, please?' said Nandini, eager to speak with Banita.

Looking at Devyani happily playing with Haripriya and Balaram, Banita said, 'Yes, sure. Just look at her. She's so happy. I think your son sharing his ice cream with the girls has done the trick.'

The ladies sat outside a juice bar, while the kids played in the open green area in front.

'My name is Nandini and I work as a freelance music teacher.'

'And my name is,' she laughed, 'Banita. And I am an Early Learning expert at Sarasvati Vidya Mandir.'

The mothers felt an immediate camaraderie sitting there together.

'How do I develop the kind of patience and self-control you demonstrated today?' asked Nandini.

'Well, as the child grows, the parents also have a lot of growing up to do. It's a gradual process. I find a lot of burnt-out parents who are stubbornly stuck with their notions of the ideal child. It's challenging for many parents to not compare the real child they have in life with the ideal child they have in mind. This comparison with other children or with the ideal notions is a big cause of frustration, which comes out in harmful ways,' answered Banita. Nandini listened on in awe.

'How can I ensure that my kids grow up to their potential?' asked Nandini further.

'Kids are sensitive people. They have to be treated with utmost patience and protected from judgemental behaviour. We don't realize it, but our verbal and non-verbal reactions can be demoralizing for them. Treated harshly for a mistake can make them feel unwanted and stupid. Then they can go to great lengths to hide their mistakes and disguise their learning challenges.'

'Learning challenges?' asked a curious Nandini.

'Do you know what dyslexia is?' asked Banita.

'I've heard the term, but I am not sure I know what it means,' came the reply.

'Well, you are not the only one. A lot of parents don't know this or think of it as a stigma. Dyslexia is an unexpected difficulty in learning to read. It is not a disease or any kind of physical or mental disability. You can say it is like a very specific learning difficulty, but it doesn't impact the child's entire brain. Devyani has dyslexia. Sure, she has struggles reading, but she is a very intelligent and creative child,' explained Banita.

'Can you tell me more about this condition?' asked Nandini further.

'Well, if my memory serves me right, according to a research done in America, one in five students has dyslexia to varying degrees. Dyslexia takes away the kid's ability to read quickly and retrieve spoken words easily. So, educators like myself need training to be able to identify it early in students so that proper learning adjustments can be made.'

'What can be done to help a child who has dyslexia?' asked Nandini.

'A lot of parents harshly think of their child as stupid because of their reading and speaking challenges. Teachers need to identify and communicate this, parents need to understand and be open-minded about this, and—most importantly—grown-up dyslexic students need to know this to deflate the suspense around it. It is nothing to be ashamed of. Dyslexia doesn't have to be an academic death sentence. It does not dampen a child's creativity or higher order thinking skills like understanding concepts, building conceptual connections and executing problem-solving or troubleshooting,' explained Banita.

'Thank you so much for sharing this with me. I think I know someone who would benefit from this information. Can I have your business card?' asked Nandini, while handing over her own business card to Banita.

'Sorry, I don't have a business card, but let me write my number for you. You are most welcome to contact me. I would love for Devyani and your children to have a play date soon. I can clearly see how much effort you have invested in raising them. They are so cultured and friendly,' said Banita, finishing her orange juice.

'And I'd like to be your friend and learn from you about being patient when my two naughty munchkins do my head in,' said Nandini as both mothers laughed out loud.

śaknotīhaiva yaḥ soḍhuṁ
prāk śarīra-vimokṣaṇāt
kāma-krodhodbhavaṁ vegaṁ
sa yuktaḥ sa sukhī naraḥ
(Bhagavad Gita 5.23)

Friends, this verse from the Gita indicates that as long as the soul is situated in a material body, our bodily condition will invite troublesome situations that will require emotional regulation. It identifies the inner forces of lust and anger as the enemies of our peace and happiness. The temptations of lust and the actions of anger are to be tolerated in order to become situated in happiness. Slavery to negative emotions is the classic cause of self-sabotage.

Both lust and anger impel us to act in many undesirable ways. Anger in particular is perhaps the only emotion that has been linked with cardiovascular risks. Angry people are prone to high blood pressure, which causes heart damage over time.

Feeling entitled to express our anger for having been wronged, it can be difficult to hold back our rage. At the same time, we want to exercise control to give a befitting response and not aggravate the situation unnecessarily. In such a dual state of accelerating emotions and attempted restraint, we put our heart under tremendous pressure. It's like stepping on the accelerator and brake of a car at the same time.

PLACE OF ANGER IN LIFE

Anger is a natural reaction. It is a spontaneous emotion that sprouts when we encounter injustice or when things that are important to us don't go the way we intended. While anger may be a justified reaction, its actions are often undesirable. What feels natural is not always desirable. How many times have we allowed our naturally arising feelings of anger to worsen the situation? Driven by anger, we may act or speak in a way that may hurt others and ourselves in the process.

But the solution is not to be passive amid injustice or display artificial repression. In fact, we may invite more trouble by not appropriately reacting to the situation. Giving in to anger, however, deludes us and takes away our intelligence. We end up overreacting and worsening the situation. An unchecked angry outburst can quickly turn the victim into a culprit.

When guided by intelligence, our anger can focus more on the problem and its solution rather than the cause of the problem (the culprit) and its faults. By responding wisely and assertively, we can address the problem itself productively and deal with the culprit constructively.

TOLERATING THE FORCES OF ANGER

Controlling our anger does not mean suppressing it. However, we all have experienced that our anger can play devil if we allow it to carry out its indiscriminate judgements. Weakened by anger, we allow situations to determine our actions rather than wisely choosing our reaction to the situation.

Maturity to deal with provocative situations comes from tolerating the force of anger. Resisting anger therefore requires strength and not everybody is born with it, but it can be cultivated. And like any strength training programme, to toughen our mental muscles of tolerance, we need to follow a specific programme:

Warm-up: Like this verse declares, bodily encasement of the soul invites constant troubles for us in this world. So let's accept reality as it is and not as we would like it to be. Warming up our mental muscles of tolerance by keeping small things small and not jumping straight into vigorous emotional deadlifts over trifles is an ideal start.

Focus on getting stronger: To gain muscle for our tolerance-muscles, we need to regularly stretch our intelligence. We begin to get stronger to handle provoking situations only by shifting our focus from our faculty of emotion (our mind) to our faculty to reason (our intelligence).

Progressive overload: By gradually increasing the weight of patience in pressing situations, we increase the capacity to tolerate even the most intense situations. Putting to use our newly developed muscles of tolerance will help us effortlessly handle recurring situations.

Consistent effort: Toughening our grip over our negative emotions is not for the faint-hearted. The tolerance game is a gradual process. It takes time to excel at it. Enjoy the ride and continually look to make small gains; they add up over time!

Repetitions and breaks: Ultimately, to not get injured during the course of our emotional training, we need access to a protective spiritual energy. Taking a break from the regular course of life to reflect on the ever-present goodwill of our coach, the Supreme Lord, we can recover from unfortunate relapses. Energized by acknowledging God's grace, we rebound quicker to continue our inner workout routines.

Nutrition: A regular diet of spiritual wisdom allows us to get rid of unhealthy emotional weight. Meditation is a far tastier and healthier replacement to the feel-good junk food of unhealthy emotions. Over and above, without deeper spiritual fulfilment, it is hard to keep away from the attractive offers of hot and sizzling emotional outbursts.

We build inner strength by following the programme above. By cultivation of spiritual strength in connection with the Supreme Lord, we can reclaim our control over anger.

THIRTY-TWO

Cheating through Profit

Human Quality: Mindfulness

Trivedi was known as 'Eco Kaka'. Having retired from the railways a few years ago, he now spent most of his time reading and gardening. Sharing his gardening skills along with the produce he grew were his hobbies. Gardening for Trivedi was a form of meditation. To engage his mind, body and spirit with the soil, water, air and sunlight was 'part of a healthy life'.

'It's a healthy workout with tasty rewards. My terrace garden is my yoga mat. It has helped me lower my blood pressure, is good for my bones and has helped me get over my addiction to my smartphone. Just being with nature lifts your mood. Your kids throw food tantrums? Grow it with them and see them develop a lasting habit of good eating.' Trivedi endlessly promoted gardening to everyone.

The early weekend mornings were a headache for Eco Kaka. The neighbourhood kids ruled the street, playing cricket all day long. No force in the universe could control them. They had slogged all week at school, waiting for the moment to now slog it on the cricket pitch on the street.

The dreaded air-drive was Trivedi's nightmare. It meant six runs for the batsman, but a sacrificed tomato, a fallen carrot, a destroyed capsicum or even worse, a broken pot for him.

Bribes of crispy vegetable samosas, rich tomato soups and tasty carrot-halva only materialized in false promises from the boys. Threats and complaints had also proved to be insufficient deterrents. Something more innovative was required. The situation required out of the box thinking.

One day, as the game reached its climax, Gali All Rounders required six runs off the last ball against Ferocious Fasties. Eco Kaka cheered for Gali All Rounders, hoping in his heart for a winning six to land in his terrace garden. The boys were surprised by this unsuspecting cheer from their 'enemy number one'. Nakul took guard as Vaasu charged in, steaming. A swing of the bat and the ball went for a six, but also took out one of Eco Kaka's lettuce pots. As the boys prepared to flee, they heard Eco Kaka clapping and celebrating the victory for the Gali All Rounders.

'What an exciting finish! I've been missing out on all this fun, boys. I guess some earthworm entered my ear and ate up the fun part of my brain,' loudly said a visibly happy Mr Trivedi. As the boys laughed at his joke, Trivedi uncle called everyone over for some chilled mango lassi and samosas.

After the refreshments, Mr Trivedi gave each boy a twenty-rupee note.

'This is your prize money. You boys play so hard and should be rewarded for the blood and the sweat, isn't that right?' remarked Eco Kaka, while insisting the boys take one more samosa each. While leaving, the boys spoke among themselves, appreciating the respect and reward they received.

Next Saturday, as the boys assembled, Mr Trivedi joined them from his balcony. The game ended, the boys were called over and served chilled mango lassi and rewarded ten rupees each with lots of encouraging words for their efforts. Looking at the ten-rupee note, the boys were unsure about their feelings and many felt doubtful about their effort in this game.

The following Saturday, the post-game refreshments at Eco Kaka's house took a further toll with only simple lemonade and five-rupee coins for everyone.

'But today was a nail-biter, better than any other game we have had in a long time. We had discussed we'd give it our all and today's effort deserved fifty rupees each! So much effort and Eco Kaka gave us this stupid five-rupee coin,' the boys discussed afterwards.

'I don't think he understood how much effort went into today's game,' said someone with a dejected look.

The following Saturday, after another cliff-hanger cricket match, the boys waited for Mr Trivedi to call them over.

'We all decided to play our hardest today, gave our 110 per cent to it and win that money we deserved, but Eco Kaka seemed to not even acknowledge our efforts today,' said Aryan. Everybody voiced their agreement while still panting and sweating.

A few minutes of anxious anticipation felt like a year to the boys as they waited for Mr Trivedi's wave of the hand.

'Why is he just looking around and not calling us over?' asked the Ferocious Fasties' captain Sarvesh.

As the boys approached, they found the entrance door closed. Mr Trivedi waved at the boys from his first-floor balcony.

'Eco Kaka, how was today's game? Govind turned it around with his hat-trick, the scorching heat couldn't slow his yorkers,' said Nilesh as everybody looked up at the balcony.

'Yes, it was such a good game . . . I had so much fun watching it. Honestly, I wait for your game every week!' replied Mr Trivedi.

'So . . . we were thinking that if something can be done, then, we were thinking, like, you know, I mean,' said Sarvesh.

'What! What were you thinking?' asked Mr Trivedi, pensively.

'Like, you know, we spend so much energy and it's hard work, you know, and you are having all the fun watching us slog it under the sun. I mean . . .' said a hesitant Vandan.

Interjecting, Mr Trivedi asked, '. . . and so you expect me to?'

'Leave it boys, he doesn't deserve this fun, I think we are simply being used for unpaid entertainment,' said Neel, who captained Gali All Rounders.

The next Saturday morning as the boys came with their cricket kits, they saw Mr Trivedi setting up his chair in the balcony. With a colourful beach shirt and dark sunglasses on, while sipping on a raw coconut, Mr Trivedi looked like he was heading for a holiday.

Both teams quickly clubbed together for what looked like a combined strategic timeout. A few moments later, they took out the stumps from the turf and moved to the far end of the neighbourhood where Mr Trivedi could neither see nor hear them. Taking his sunglasses off, Eco Kaka looked on with a blank expression, giving an un-tasteful send-off to the teams.

And in this way, what appeared to be an offer for reward ultimately became the cause of diminishing enthusiasm from the perspective of the kids. The terrace garden never saw a broken pot again. Eco Kaka had won!

lobhaḥ pravṛttir ārambhaḥ
karmaṇām aśamaḥ spṛhā
rajasy etāni jāyante
vivṛddhe bharataṛṣabha
(Bhagavad Gita 14.12)

Friends, this informative verse from the fourteenth chapter of the Gita illuminates the effect of Passion (*Rajas*) on our consciousness. Passion clouds our consciousness with a disproportionate desire for gain and can make us greedy. A restless sense of hankering develops as a result and an unhealthy sense of attachment becomes visible in our behaviour. The net outcome of Rajas is an underlying sense of dissatisfaction despite all that we have. In short, Rajas makes us over-endeavour, leaves us always wanting more and makes us feel miserable.

Influenced by Rajas, the neighbourhood boys became driven to get rewarded for what they used to enjoy earlier. Passion planted a sense of entitlement in them. Incentive thus killed their enthusiasm as greed for reward overwhelmed their minds. While earlier they were happy playing their game without any strings attached, once they started chasing a reward for it, they were bound up by increasing feelings of dissatisfaction.

KNOW YOUR INFLUENCERS

Yoga texts like the Gita help us develop an understanding of ourselves, the world around us and our own individual realities in it. By helping us better understand the subtle environmental forces that affect our consciousness, the Gita helps us prepare, navigate and seek the best outcomes in every situation.

The material environment has three primary effects influencing our consciousness. They are *Sattva*, *Rajas* and *Tamas* or influences of Goodness, Passion and Darkness. These three subtle forces affect our consciousness and subsequently our thoughts, words and deeds. Identifying when we are being influenced by the moods of material nature can motivate us, help us and even save us.

In contrast to Rajas, Sattva or Goodness has an elevating effect on our consciousness. It increases our awareness and inspires satisfaction in us by engaging us in positive thoughts and deeds. While Passion drives us to *just do it*, Goodness helps us plan and organize beforehand. When our inner thermostat is set to Sattva, we focus better, feel internally well-grounded and are set to the ideal temperature for learning new things.

Finally, Tamas or Darkness makes us slumberous, careless and negligent. Procrastination, lethargy, self-harm, delusion, daydreaming with no outcome are some of the prominent external effects when we have our consciousness set to Tamas.

SATTVA, RAJAS, TAMAS AND ONTOLOGICAL DESIGN

It is no secret that these environmental energies shape who we are. Places can have an effect on our consciousness. Stepping into a library can trigger focus and contemplative thoughts within us, whereas stepping into a wedding hall arouses feelings of celebration. Remember the feeling of serendipity and calm experienced at a house of worship?

Alongside our external environments having an effect on us, each of our sensory experiences can also make us feel a certain way. Different genres of music make us feel differently; diverse cuisines induce feelings distinctive from each other.

Heavy metal or punk rock music colours our consciousness with frenzied sensations, while soothing flute music has a de-stressing and relaxing effect on us. Similarly, alcohol and other intoxicants, which are primarily by their constitutional nature Tamas.

All this is because everything we experience has its constitutional nature rooted in a mix of the three influences of the material environment—Goodness, Passion and Darkness.

In the field of design philosophy, the concept of ontological design has been gathering momentum. Ontological design explains that what we create externally, creates us internally too. We are being actively designed by the surroundings we live in, the tools and phone applications we use, the music we hear and the food we eat. What we consume and create, creates and consumes us in return. There is a constant feedback loop going.

PROGRAMMING YOUR ENVIRONMENT

Friends, it should not come as a surprise to you that we programme our environment to facilitate the actions that we intend to pursue. But how, you may ask? We already understand that Sattva increases our awareness, Rajas makes us driven with impulses and Tamas hinders our awareness.

If you leave your room messy, with stacks of paper and books lying everywhere, an untidy bed, a rubbish bin full to the brim with rotten banana peels from last week and dirty clothes lying everywhere on the floor, you have pretty much created a room full of obstacles, negative energy and chaos. In short, you have set the environmental thermostat of your room to Tamas.

In such a room, Tamas will make sure that you don't feel comfortable with all sorts of things getting in the way of your goals. You'll feel nervous in there all the time and continue to act out of Darkness, procrastinating and reacting slowly to important and even urgent matters. Instead, by keeping your room tidy, you activate Sattva and as a result, better organize your thoughts and better execute your plans.

While Rajas is required for goals that necessitate hard work, Sattva is still your best friend to help you contemplate these goals first and maintain focus throughout.

Tamas is also very useful. It is meant to slow you down and induce you to take a break. It is required to get good quality sleep. But when that Tamas is contaminated by the Rajas-inducing bright screen light from your smartphone, you can be assured of a restless night.

RISING UP AND GOING BEYOND

Yoga texts not only guide us on how to better set up productive environments and how to internally acclimatize ourselves to environments beyond our control, but also how to altogether surpass these subtle natural forces.

The transcendental process of bhakti-yoga helps us rise above these forces and situates us in the most desirable position where we feel the most happy, peaceful and productive with our life. But these are only the fringe benefits of bhakti-yoga. Its real benefit is the revival of our forgotten loving relationship with Krishna or the Supreme Lord.

THIRTY-THREE

Selfishness Is Self-Destructive

Human Quality: Friendship

Lallu, Lambu and Lallan were a notorious trio of criminals. Their hideouts were deep within the unknown mountain ranges of central India.

Lambu was strongly built and used to be a promising wrestler in his village. After losing a land dispute to his elder brother, he had turned violent and full of vengeance. Attacking his brother's family, he fled his village thinking he had killed his brother's wife during a tussle with him. The lady had later recovered, but Lambu in hiding was unaware of it. He had struggled with his conscience to deal with the blood he now thought he had on his hands. Thinking of no path to return to civil society, he had jumped headfirst into a criminal life, specializing in extortion for the local land mafia.

Lallan, on the other hand, was very intelligent and the son of a wealthy man. His polite and handsome demeanour was quite contrary to the criminal life he led. Through terrible company, he had become addicted to gambling and wine. Ruining the good name of his family, Lallan had run away and took to a life of crime when his father had decided to put him in a correction and drug rehabilitation facility. Seeking revenge for 'life's injustice' through crime was a downward spiral Lallan had jumped into.

The third and most dangerous of the trio was Lallu. Although a petty thief at the start, he was now a dreaded criminal in the region. As is with a life of crime, Lallu's frequent catch-ups with other jailbirds had strengthened his ambition for antisocial behaviour. From a pickpocket to an armed robber, Lallu's progressive degradation had been quick and dangerous.

It was the new moon night and the Lallu-Lambu-Lallan gang was carrying out the largest jewellery heist in the city's history. Broad-shouldered Lambu tackled the store's security guard and knocked him out. Lallan kept an eye out for the police, while Lallu used his intelligence and skills to break open the store.

Once inside, the trio worked with precision. Lallan cleared the jewellery displays, while Lambu and Lallu used gunpowder explosives to open the main safe. In a matter of twenty minutes, the trio was out with bag-loads of valuables. Two horses were ridden through the dark alley up to the edge of the river. From there, the trio travelled on foot to the dangerously dense part of the forest.

'It's dangerous to carry any of this money and jewels with us. Now, as per the plan, let us bury everything here at this spot between these tall teak trees,' said Lallan.

'Lallan, what a detailed plan you hatched. We've hit the jackpot! Yes, let us bury everything. Here, let me help you dig that pit,' offered Lambu, smiling and flexing his big muscles.

'Boys, we should not be seen together for some time. Once things settle down, we will meet again to divide this wealth and move overseas,' said Lallu with penetrating bloodshot eyes.

'Lambu, mark that tree over there with that sharp stone and we are done,' said Lallan.

Sweating but excited, the trio lay down on the floor of the forest.

'Who else is hungry?' asked Lallu a little while later.

'I am!' said the other two robbers almost in sync.

'Let me grab some food. I'll be back in an hour. In a few weeks, we'll be served hot meals like kings,' said a smirking Lallu.

It is said that the influence of bad money quickly changes minds. With Lallu away, Lambu and Lallan devised a nefarious plan while still sitting atop the buried treasure chest.

'We both come from reputed families and can turn our image around. Lallu, on the other hand, is a seasoned criminal. He loves the criminal life and has deep connections with much darker forces. As for this wealth, we can claim to have received a family inheritance. We can live a life of comfort and pleasure. Lallu is a misfit for our public image,' said Lallan.

'I am with you on this. This is our golden opportunity. We have the money and we have each other's support. I want to go back home, get married, raise a family and serve my old parents who still long for me,' said Lambu in his deep voice.

'I want to do the same. But for this, that criminal Lallu has to be removed from our path,' said Lallan with conviction as he fixed his gaze on a thorny bush nearby.

Meanwhile, away to get food, Lallu wasn't thinking very differently from his partners in crime.

'These city boys do not deserve this fortune. It was I who broke into the store. It was my skills that helped open the metal safe. That spoiled kid Lallan is always jumping up and down, barking orders at me. And that beast of man, Lambu, he has zero imagination and is dull like a stone. They both are misfits for this life of adventure. They are both alcoholics and may let their guard down in public while drunk. They cannot be trusted. They have to die.' Deciding thus, the poison of his mind manifested in a bottle in his pocket. Lallu mixed the poison with the food and started back for the forest.

Back at the buried treasure site in the deep forest, Lallu saw Lambu resting on his back with his hands under his head.

'Where is Lallan?' asked Lallu while placing the food parcel on a big rock slab.

'Here is Lallan!' yelled Lallan, grabbing Lallu's neck from the back and strangling his victim, who tried to resist but failed in the two-against-one contest.

'Goodbye Lallu, we will miss you,' said Lambu as he grabbed Lallu's feet, who struggled to get free while Lallan strangled him. It was a gruesome sight.

'We will take these empty jewellery bags and drown him in the river. People will think he robbed the store, but drowned while getting away and lost his loot to the fast-flowing waters,' said Lallan.

'That's a great plan! Let's do it. Sunrise is still a few hours away,' said Lambu, as he picked up the lifeless body of Lallu on his shoulders like a hunter carrying a dead fox. Lallan hung the backpack of tools they had used on his left shoulder and picked up the food parcel with his right hand.

Once at the river shore, Lambu put the dead body down, while Lallan worked on fixing 'proofs' on it. He tucked a few empty jewellery bags into Lallu's pockets. As a proof to be found on his body, he tied a bag with gold coins to Lallu's waist belt. The two men then disposed of Lallu's body.

'Goodbye, Lallu. Have a safe journey,' said Lallan, waving to Lallu's dead body as the river's fast stream carried it away.

'Lambu, let's leave. We don't want to be seen anywhere near here.'

'Where shall we go?' asked Lambu.

'I know a bar on the other side of the village. Through the southern side of the forest we can reach there unseen by the city guards. We will get drunk there and make ourselves visible to the people. No one will then think of us as having anything to do with last night's city robbery,' said Lallan.

'I know that bar! But that route you are suggesting will be too long. I know a shortcut; we have to reach the bar before sunrise,' said Lambu.

'Great, let's get going,' Lallan said, as he passed on the food pack to Lambu and fixed the backpack of tools on both his shoulders.

Deep into an unknown side of the forest, Lallan followed Lambu's lead. A little while later, Lallan stopped for a quick break, catching his breath.

'We have to walk faster Lallan, if we wish to make it to the bar in time,' said Lambu.

'I understand we must reach there before the day breaks, but this heavy tool bag is really slowing me down,' replied Lallan.

'Let me take it off you and you carry this lighter food pack,' said Lambu.

'Thanks, Lambu,' said Lallan with a smile of relief.

But as Lambu went behind Lallan to take the backpack off him, he grabbed Lallan's neck between his mighty biceps.

'Lallan, both you and that Lallu always ridiculed me as a beast of burden who "couldn't add one plus one". Isn't it surprising that I am now executing one minus one! I know you both would cheat me and distribute the wealth unequally. Without me, you guys were nothing, but you never gave me the respect I deserved,' said Lambu as he tightened his grip around Lallan's neck. Lallan tried to free himself desperately but failed, gasping.

After strangulating Lallan to death, and digging and burying his body in a pit, Lambu sat down, pleased with himself.

'Sunrise is still an hour away. I'll still make it to that bar, but I'm feeling so hungry. After all, parting from dear friends is a very traumatic and exhausting experience,' said Lambu to himself, laughing as he sat on a stone slab nearby while opening the food pack.

Halfway into his meal, the hard-hearted murderer felt as if something was choking his neck. It was the poison Lallu had smeared in the food. Lambu struggled for air and fell down dead while jackals cried in the background.

> kiṃ mitramante sukṛtaṃ na lokāḥ
> kiṃ dhyeyamīśasya padaṃ na śokāḥ ।
> kiṃ kāmyamavyājasukhaṃ na bhogāḥ
> kiṃ jalpanīyaṃ harināma nānyat ॥

Friends, this great poetic composition presents some fascinating rhetorical questions for us to ponder.

kiṃ mitramante: At the end, who is our true friend? Our good deeds (*sukṛtam*), not necessarily people (*lokāḥ*).

kiṃ dhyeyam: What is worthy of our contemplation? Not sorrowful life events, not missed opportunities and not the inescapable pain of worldly existence (*śokāḥ*). Real solace can be found in meditation on the two lotus feet of the Supreme Lord (*īśasya padaṃ*).

kiṃ kāmyam: What is truly worth pursuing in life? Not the fleeting and costly happiness of the ephemeral world (*bhogāḥ*), but by spiritualizing our consciousness, the costless and increasing joy of spirituality (*avyāja-sukhaṃ*).

kiṃ jalpanīyaṃ: And what is truly worth repeating with our tongue? Not passing news or useless gossip. Without question, it is the holy name of Hari (*hari-nāma na anyat*). Hari is a specific name of the Supreme Divine who removes both inner and outer obstacles of all those who connect with that Divine Lord through sonic meditation on the holy names of God.

The answers proposed in the verse are thoughtful conclusions of sages who have considered both the temporary nature of the material existence and the permanent existence of the spiritual dimension.

OUR DEEDS AS OUR TRUE FRIENDS

We all need real friends in life. As much as we would like them to be unconditionally supportive of us and dedicated to our growth, an experienced fact of our lives is that our search for a true friend takes us through many disappointing candidates.

We come across friends who may be unable to help us. Others may even be unwilling to help, despite their resources and proximity to us. Some friends may not stand with us or may sign a cheque of 'sorry' in times most needed. Worse yet, we come across 'friends' who are keen to cheat us or use us to their benefit.

Among all these 'friends', we should be grateful to true well-wishers who are always there for us, unconditionally accepting of us with all our flaws. Sadly, often they do not know how to help us improve our lives without imposing themselves on us. Nonetheless, it is only wise to walk away from greedy liars like Lallu, narcissistic schemers like Lallan and fake helpful people like Lambu. People addicted to bad habits can never be anybody's true friend. They are dangerous to our peace, progress and well-being.

The sages propose in this verse that our true friend in this world is our own good actions. Our deeds reward us, like a capable, appreciative and loving friend. Our deeds punish us, like a selfless friend not hesitating to reprimand us when we go off track. Our deeds build us, like a loyal friend dedicated to our growth in life. Our deeds never hesitate to show us the mirror of our own lacking or overdoing. It is our deeds alone that stand by us through our success and failure in this life and beyond.

THIRTY-FOUR

Power of Obedience

Human Quality: Submissiveness

Joydeb Goswami was a respected priest at the large Doul Govinda temple in north Guwahati. He had been trying to inspire Udoy, a local woodcutter, to deal with the stresses found in forestry by taking his spiritual practices seriously.

'Goswamiji, you have no idea how dangerous the forest is,' Udoy would often repeatedly complain.

'Yes Udoy, there is danger at every step; we need to be careful and vigilant. But know this, no one is alone in this forest of material existence. The Lord is always within our hearts! Simply by calling out His names with devotion, you can invoke His presence. Just try this with faith and see how it helps you deal with what troubles your mind,' Joydeb would often reply to Udoy.

'Goswamiji, please don't make things difficult for me. I have no time for all this. Just pray for me and give me your blessings,' Udoy would request.

'Why don't you come to the temple every Sunday? Attend the aarti ceremony and hear the Gita. You will gain spiritual strength and knowledge. It will help you put a context to your fears,' the priest would further request.

'Sunday is my rest day. I cannot come on Sunday. I have to work so hard, so Sunday is God's gift to me.' In this way, Udoy would excuse himself from any suggestions made by the priest and insist that the priest simply give him blessings of gain, protection and fearlessness.

'God helps all, but especially those who help themselves stay connected with Him! You have to do something to control your mind, the sitting place for fear. God's divine names are the most potent way to control the mind. Unless you have something positive to turn on, you will never be able to turn off the negative,' the priest would conclude. However, Udoy was of the mindset of putting in zero effort and choosing passive solutions to his problems.

Once, at the temple, Udoy repeated his tale of fears. The priest had an idea. Realizing that the woodcutter had an unnatural fear and unwillingness to make any effort to deal with it, the priest thought of engaging him positively to give him something to hang on to when his panic was triggered in the forest.

'Udoy, do you know who Chakradev is?' the priest asked.

'Yes, Chakradev is my neighbour. He's our local potter.'

'Exactly. I have a very easy solution to help you win over your fears,' proposed Joydeb.

'Only if it is easy. Tell me, Goswamiji.'

'It's very easy, Udoy. It will not just protect you and help you overcome your fears, but also invoke the special mercy of the Lord on you,' replied the priest.

'Tell me, tell me, Goswamiji,' responded Udoy with excitement.

'Every day before you leave for the forest, ensure you see your neighbour and as soon as you see him, speak out his name three times,' proposed the priest.

'And this will protect me? Wow, this is simple. You have finally given me something that is doable for me,' said Udoy, nodding in agreement.

'Yes, it will help you in more ways than you think, my friend. But you must do this with faith, making this your first regulation in life,' said the priest, thinking about the real meaning of the word chakradev, 'the Lord who carries a disc weapon to protect His devotees'.

In this way, the priest induced Udoy to call out the name of the Lord for his protection and well-being.

Following this regulation every day, Udoy would climb upon his fence, see the potter working on the potter's wheel, speak out his name thrice and set out to the forest. This became his daily routine. After few weeks of this practice, the woodcutter started feeling a sense of satisfaction and protection in his heart because he was putting his faith in a higher authority.

One day, Udoy had to leave for the forest early. It was before his regular time. He came to his fence, but could not find Chakradev at his potter's wheel.

Anxious, Udoy became nervous and thought, 'I am going into the denser part of the forest today. Without seeing the potter, how can I call his name and be assured of protection?'

Thinking like this, Udoy climbed down on the other side of the fence and started looking for the potter. While quietly looking for him, Udoy heard some digging noises. Behind the dirt wall, Chakradev was digging for mud, but had unearthed something that he wasn't expecting. It was a pot filled with gold coins! Shocked and excited, Chakradev looked around anxiously to see if anybody had spotted him with the newfound treasure. Just right at that moment, Udoy had come up and found him digging for dirt, unaware of the pot of gold Chakradev was holding.

'Chakradev! Chakradev! Chakradev! I've seen Chakradev!' Udoy exclaimed out of happiness for having sighted the potter and now ensured in his heart of protection in the forest. In a frenzy of excitement, unaware of the gold Chakradev was holding in the pot, Udoy started running back to his fence still calling out loudly, 'Chakradev! Chakradev! Chakradev! I've seen Chakradev!'

Seeing Udoy running away, the potter got suspicious and cried out, 'Hey! What happened? What did you see?'

'I have seen, I have seen and I have nothing to fear!' responded Udoy frantically as he ran.

Becoming suspicious and thinking about Udoy's response, Chakradev thought to himself, 'The woodcutter says he has seen and that he has nothing to fear. Now he will tell the whole village and my newfound fortune will be put under dispute.'

Immediately, Chakradev called out to Udoy, 'Brother Udoy, I know you have seen me and that you have nothing to fear. I know you have nothing to lose either, but you definitely have a lot to gain. What if we share this fifty-fifty?'

'Fifty-fifty?' thought Udoy, trying to make sense of what Chakradev was saying.

Stopping and turning around, Udoy looked on as Chakradev pulled him inside his hut and showed him the pot he was covering under a cloth.

'Stop yelling immediately and do not tell any of this to anyone. Let us divide this gold I have found buried in my backyard among ourselves. Then like you, I too will have nothing to fear. You'll be happy and I'll be happy,' said Chakradev as he unveiled the pot with its precious gold coins shining inside.

Awestruck, Udoy thought to himself, 'I have simply followed the word of a saintly figure, although instead of following his real advice, I got him to sanction what I wanted to do. My fear went away and now I have been rewarded so handsomely. What if I actually followed what he earlier advised by his own accord about serving at the temple and learning the Gita?'

tāvad bhayeṣu bhetavyaṁ
yāvadbhayamanāgatam
āgataṁ tu bhayaṁ dṛṣṭvā
prahartavyama śaṅkayā

Friends, this is a verse by Acharya Chanakya on fear. He is suggesting that fear can act both as a protective shield against dangers and as an attacking launchpad to win over our weaknesses. As an indicator of danger, fear can alert and protect us. Fear can also help us identify our weaknesses. It can give us opportunities to prepare and build ourselves up.

Fear serves us constructively when we rise up to face it with resolute determination.

WHAT IS THE CAUSE OF FEAR?

Woody Allen famously said, 'I'm not afraid of death; I just don't want to be there when it happens.' Self-preservation is an existential feature of all forms of life, even those without any self-awareness like a virus. Yoga wisdom explains that the instinct of self-preservation is rooted in the spiritual nature of the soul. If life is meaningless and there is nothing after death, then why should death matter to us at all? If we are only a bundle of dead atoms, why don't we opt to not respond to dangers? Should it make a difference if a heap of atoms is dismantled? If we carry no intrinsic value, why at all do we seek to live forever or are afraid to even talk about death?

Unlike its material bodily covering which is inert matter (*asat*), unaware of itself (*achid*) and dull (*niraanand*), the soul is eternal (*sat*), cognizant (*chid*) and pleasure-seeking (*ananda*). We don't see a dead rat experiencing fear of a cat or pleasure at the prospect of a cheesy reward. The materially embodied soul experiences fear in the mind when it becomes aware (*chid*) of danger to either its bodily existence (*sat*) or the sources of its happiness (*ananda*).

By taking our body to be our real self, we unwittingly outsource our happiness to external things, things which are not always under our control. Through material things and material experiences, we enjoy some pleasure. As a result, we become attached to them. Our experience further teaches us that all things material have an expiry date. Thus, attached to material things that give us happiness and aware of losing them either to time or circumstances beyond our control, we become fearful. Through the possibility of losing them or their inevitable destruction, the very things that give us pleasure become a source of our fear and insecurities.

In a nutshell, our material misidentification causes us fear and our material desires bind us to fear.

HOW CAN WE WIN OVER OUR FEARS?

As explained by Joydeb Goswami to Udoy in this story, the mind is the sitting place of fear inside us. The same mind that has an unlimited capacity to paint dark dystopian pictures of the future or the unknown. To win over our fears, we need to win over our mind.

Paralysed by fear of the future and handicapped by the pain of the past, we may not be able to respond in the present to situations that intimidate us. At such times, we need to get off the mind's rollercoaster and deal with the present as it is. Remember, reality is often not as bad as the mind's projection of it.

Needless to say, it helps to identify real dangers from those imagined by our fearful mind. Overwhelmed by fear, our mind clogs our vision, cripples our decision-making and curtails our response to difficult situations. To be able to see things clearly, we need inner clarity. Pranayama or yogic breathing exercises help calm the mind and ground it in the present to see things more clearly.

Practically dealing with fear needs the help of our intelligence. We need our intelligence, and not our mind, in the driver's seat. The mind generates emotions; the intelligence should make our decisions. We need to learn this distinction. When our intelligence drives our responses, we make properly deliberated decisions and are able to act on them. When our mind drives our responses, it makes us lazy, crazy and sometimes sleazy.

BECOMING FEARLESS

While tolerating our fears depends on the strength of our mind and appropriately dealing with them depends on the strength of our intelligence, transcending our fears depends on the strength of our spiritual wisdom.

That everything material is temporary and bends in front of gravity is known to all. How then can one ever seek to rise to the high skies where worldly problems do not chase and scare us any more?

By cultivation of our dormant spirituality, we access strength that lies beyond the limitations of our body and mind. The ageless soul, an indestructible being, untouched by any of the material forces of the universe, seeks to redeem itself through its own spiritual power. On its multi-life journey of spiritual evolution, as the soul revives its existential relationship with its source, God, it becomes proportionately free from the material chains of fear and frustration.

Thus, by cultivating our awareness of our immortal spiritual nature and depending on our ever-well-wishing Lord, we access the protective grace that gives us real strength to face all our fears.

By adopting genuine wisdom cultures like the bhakti tradition and by practising authentic spirituality like the path of bhakti-yoga, we can experience our living connection with God. As this relationship grows stronger, the practitioner experiences a natural shift of focus from the mind's fears to the heart's faith. Faith in the supremely competent and omni-benevolent Lord, ever ready to help and protect us.

THIRTY-FIVE

Funny Justice

Human Quality: Self-Control

Murli, the local cowherd, was a simple-hearted man. He shared a special relationship with each of his cows. The cows knew their own names and responded by mooing when Murli would call them lovingly. During feeding or milking times, Murli would have elaborate talks with them or narrate to them stories from the Ramayana and the Mahabharata. Often at such times, some of the cows would stretch their necks for Murli to rub and in an exchange of affection, would lick him back.

'My dear girls, I have heard that the sages say that rivers are the veins of the planet. Sadly, we have no rivers flowing in our region. This ground water therefore is mother earth's arrangement for us poor folks who are not so fortunate to live near a sacred river,' he would explain to his cows, who would look at him with inquisitive eyes hoping to be fed a banana or a carrot.

Always concerned for his cows' welfare, Murli had been saving for over two years to buy a sweet water well near his farm, which was owned by a wealthy horse rancher, Premanjan.

Pongal was a few weeks away, but it felt like the festival of joy had come early this year for Murli. He had just signed the deed of agreement with Premanjan and handed over the money he had been saving to buy the well for his cow farm. With the deal settled, Murli joyfully rushed home to share the news with his family. Once back, he went straight to the cowshed to see his beloved cows. Talking animatedly, he explained to them his plans for their new well.

'I will engage your powerful husbands, the mighty bulls, to draw fresh water for you. These powerful bulls won't fight anymore and scare people. They will finally get to flex their muscles for a good reason. My dear cows, now you will get to watch your babies have plenty of water sports events.'

Murli turned to Harini while her calf drank her milk, 'Harini, now you girls will have as much water to drink as you like, even during the hot summers. Your precious milk will flow like a pure river. And like you, I too will not keep this nectar to myself. You supply more milk than the calves need and share the remaining milk with us. I will also share the well's nectar of sweet water with the needy. Just see, God's gift is more than our needs!' And like this, Murli continued soliloquizing while caressing his pet cows for hours together.

Next day, as Murli went to collect the first lot of water from the well, Premanjan's guards had a message for him.

'You cannot take water from the well,' the guards declared boldly.

'Are you not aware that I have purchased this well from your boss?' asked Murli, annoyed.

Just then, Premanjan stepped on the porch of his ranch and replied with a faint smile.

'Exactly, I sold you the well, not the water. And therefore, you cannot take the water. The well walls are yours to use. You may dry cow dung patties there or tie your calves there in the shade. But water you cannot draw. That is not mentioned in the deed and you have no claim on it. Are we clear on that?'

Shocked, Murli immediately contacted his good friend Bhuvnesh, who managed another big farm. After consulting a local lawyer on the matter, Bhuvnesh asked Murli to raise a dispute in the court of law.

After much back and forth, their case came up for hearing in front of the local judge. The judge, Mr Ranganathanan, heard both the parties patiently. Understanding the crookedness of the wealthy horse trader, the judge spoke to him.

'Premanjan Ji, I see that you have omitted to mention the water of the well in the deed since it was prepared by you. The illiterate Murli has only a thumbprint on it, so he had no way to figure this out. But I see your point. One interpretation of this deed could be that you have only sold the well and not the water,' said the judge in an agreeable tone.

'Exactly, Your Honour,' responded Premanjan, hardly containing the smirk on his face.

'Now, I also understand that you wish to continue taking the water of the well to maintain your horses while expecting Murli to use only the well walls. Is that so?' asked the judge further.

'Yes, Your Honour. Brother Murli is welcome to sometimes use my large water bucket to milk the cows. We will even happily pay him if he sends us some milk for our goodwill,' said the rancher while holding his hands as if promising his life away.

'Hmm, I have heard both sides, have taken into cognizance your remarks and the clauses of law on the matter. Premanjan Ji, in order for you to take water from this well, you have to do either of two things,' the judge leaned forward in his chair as he prepared to explain his decision to Premanjan.

'One, pay a monthly rent decided by the owner of the well for taking the water out of his well compound. Let me elaborate in language that you understand. Premanjan ji, to have access to the well's water, you have to have access to the well compound first and the owner of the well is in his rights to charge you a fee to use his property. Does this make sense?'

'But your honour . . .' interjected Premanjan.

Clearing his throat, the judge spoke further, 'Don't like this option? Never mind, if you are unwilling to pay an ongoing rent, then there is another option for you. You may take out all the water of the well at once since the well owner may decide to build a roof on top of his well at any time.'

Directing a penetrating gaze at Premanjan, Judge Ranganathanan concluded in a strict tone, 'I hope you understand what I mean and I hope I won't see such breaches of trust from you again!'

Realizing that his attempt to cheat has been outsmarted, Premanjan felt ashamed, while the illiterate cowherd Murli started dancing like one of his cows let out of their barn for the spring.

> *prāpyāpadam vyathate na kadācit*
> *udyogamni vicchatica apramattah*
> *dukham ca kāle sahate mahātmā*
> *dhurandharastasya jitāh sapatnāh*
> (Vidura Niti)

Friends, this verse explains a winner's mindset. Life is never easy or goes as we expect. To win in life, we need to be tough to win over our adversaries; first within ourselves and then outside of ourselves.

This verse tells us that we should not lose heart or give up in the face of difficulties and challenges. Rather, we should put up an honest fight to overcome whatever or whoever tries to hold us down. This requires us to learn to endure pain and bear the weight of responsibility to grow as per the need of the situation.

One who is willing to face up to changing circumstances, enduring the pain that change brings and shouldering the responsibility to develop through challenges, is guaranteed to win in life.

CHANGE, NOT A CHOICE

Entropy ensures that the world is always changing. We would all like for our lives to develop into something good; we wish for our relationships to sweeten over time, our careers to have an upward trajectory and we wish for the world to be a better place than yesterday. But all of this takes more than wishful thinking.

The force of time works inevitably on every aspect of our existence, on our strengths and also on our weaknesses. If we do not actively participate in our inner development, then time will make us stale and gravity will pull us down. Our small unaddressed bad habits fed with the passing of time grow into unstoppable destructive forces over years. A small misunderstanding left unheeded can cause lifelong bitterness in our heart. The inertia of inactivity can be worse than death.

By far, in most people's life, the biggest mistake made is choosing not to respond to a situation, a habit or an opportunity. Fear, comfort, lethargy, indifference, distraction; these are some of the reasons that inhibit a proper response from us. The cost of not acting far exceeds the discomfort of choosing to muster an appropriate response well within our capacity. The decision is ours; we can choose to change or be helplessly changed in ways we won't like.

SMALL IS SIGNIFICANT, DECIDE ON IT

For better or worse, change begins with a decision. The lack of a decision does not keep things suspended in a neutral state; it bears its own fruit in due course. Not reacting to life's situations is again a choice we make. This is often due to overwhelming feelings of helplessness, depression or fear of the unknown.

Deciding to make a change is an act of courage. Putting our decision-making ability into an actionable plan is valuable and rewarding. An attempt to overcome our weaknesses is a sure sign of strength. It is significant, howsoever small the step may be. Failure on the way is again a testimony that we are actually living and not just consuming oxygen. Life offers us daily opportunities to pick ourselves up and build ourselves up.

Turning possibility into reality is one of the greatest superpowers we humans have been endowed with. So remember, our decisions decide who we become and how we become and indecision is a decision.

CHANGE PERSPECTIVE TO CHANGE PURPOSE

Our motivations to act are based on our governing conceptions of life. When we believe that we are just evolutionary chunks of matter, here-today-gone-tomorrow, we inevitably come to believe in materialism as the source of our happiness. Such a perspective on life leads to increasingly self-centred choices.

Like Premanjan, when we employ our resources to collect more of the same even at the expense of others, the pursuit of resource-centred happiness supersedes the pursuit of other nobler purposes in life. A possessive mentality replaces money or other things that are functional necessities to be the very purpose of our existence. Then, money and possessions become the very basis of our self-identity and self-worth, as if they are the only source of our happiness. As a result, such a worldview warps our vision and distorts our values, turning us oblivious to the needs, pains and pleasures of others.

Change, as petitioned by the exploited victims of such a society, seeks equal or better distribution of its resources. But the situation cannot improve since no one is willing to let go of their source of happiness in life. Sadly, a materialistic worldview places material enjoyment as life's only source of happiness.

SPIRITUAL PERSPECTIVE FOR HIGHER CHANGE

The spiritual perspective offered by yoga texts like the Gita explains how equating our material existence with the complete totality of reality is a false conception of life. It is only partial reality. According to yoga wisdom, we have a dual level of existence—material and spiritual. The material is associated with the body and the mind. The spiritual with our spiritual essence, the soul.

Essentially, we all are spiritual beings currently existing in a material setting. Ignorant of our innate spirituality, we keep looking for lasting happiness through temporary material means. Everything and everyone is connected with the Supreme Source, God or Krishna, and by understanding our spiritual nature and reconnecting with our source, we come to find real happiness. This allows us to harmonize with the higher spiritual purpose of life—to love and serve God and every one of His creations. In such a spiritually purposeful life, the inner wealth that such service brings us rids us of the unhealthy cravings for the temporary. It enables us to develop the strength of character that inspires loving, trusting relationships that money can never purchase.

THIRTY-SIX

Service in Anticipation

Human Quality: Service Attitude

Parsu owned a small piece of land in a village near Ranchi. He and his son Daauji would cultivate their field and were happy with their simple life. Balli was a rich landowner. He had a big plot of land right next to Parsu's field. Balli had recently been approached by a factory owner to buy his land for setting up a shoe factory there. He was offered a very good rate, but the owner was unaware that a small cut of that land did not belong to Balli, but to Parsu.

Balli had approached Parsu to sell his field to him. The plan was to acquire Parsu's small field for a cheap rate and then approach the factory owners for the sale of the entire site. Parsu had politely declined the offer as it was not fairly priced and would rather take away their permanent source of income.

'Balli Babu, I do not want to move out of this village. This land was gifted to my grandfather by the then prince. It has fed my family and holds a sacred place in my heart.' Realizing that the meagre sum offered would run out in a few months and would effectively turn Daauji into a factory slave, Parsu had thought it wise not to pay heed to Balli's proposal.

Dishonest at heart, Balli's greed turned vicious. Conspiring, unknown to the father-son duo, on a false accusation, Balli got his associate to get Daauji arrested during the cultivation season. His plan was to stop Parsu and Daauji from cultivating that year, which would increase their debt, thus forcing them to sell their land to him at an even cheaper rate than what he had initially offered.

With the cultivation season on and his strong arms in the jail, Parsu felt depressed. Although he tried, his old body was incapable of tilling the land. In debt already, there was no way to hire labour for digging the field. Parsu was hoping that Daauji could come home soon so they could begin their work.

'My dear Daauji, it is the season to plant potatoes, but since you are not here, I am afraid we are looking at a dry future. If your mother were alive, she and I would have tried to plant something lighter together. I approached Balli Babu with a request for work at his farm to earn my meals, but he explained that, at present, he had no work for me. He was so kind that he sent a sack of rice to our house later that day. God bless him. I am also praying that God gives us the required strength and intelligence to deal with this situation,' he wrote in a letter he sent to Daauji in jail.

'Respected Pitaji, do not dig that field this year! I had hidden a gun there. In jail, I have learnt that the new collector sahib of our region is a very strict man. I don't know how he found out about my buried shotgun. I think that's why I got arrested. If only the collector sahib knew how we have to defend our field from the vicious fence that surrounds it, he would have empathized with us,' wrote Daauji in his response letter from jail.

Early next morning, a police raid was carried out at Parsu's house. A team of five policemen, headed by the district collector, stormed into the house. Another team of a dozen policemen was directed to dig up the entire field to find the hidden shotgun.

In spite of their best efforts, the team of policemen could not find any gun, neither hidden in the house nor buried in the field. They had obviously read Daauji's letter sent from the prison to his father. The collector interrogated Parsu, who pleaded that his only son had been taken away on some false accusation. The officer understood that Parsu was just an old farmer under debt, desperate in his son's absence. Parsu appeared innocently ignorant about the 'vicious fence that surrounded their field', but explained that their neighbour Balli was a kind man. He described how Balli had wanted to buy their field and was now supporting Parsu with a little food in this time of crisis. The wise collector could read Daauji's hidden message between the lines. He understood this could be a conspiracy that Balli could have hatched. Promising that he would personally investigate the matter, he left to greet an early good morning to Balli.

During the day, Parsu wrote another letter to Daauji, 'My dear son, I don't know what you are up to. First you got arrested, now there was a police raid at home! They have dug up the field looking for something and were talking about some dangerous fence. I am afraid you have been keeping your old man in dark. Please explain what is going on.'

Daauji wrote back, 'Respected Pitaji, the collector sahib met me at my jail cell after the raid they carried out at our home. He asked me to write to you and inform you that he understood what's going on with our fence and that no guns will be required to defend it. But do not mention anything to anyone at the moment.

'Father, you are a respectable man. Do not live on the charity of others. Feed that bag of rice to birds and ants. The land has been tilled for you by the state police officers; enjoy the plantation season and grow your own food! I have done what I could to serve you from inside the prison. We are grateful to the state police for their service, vigilance and dedication. The collector sahib is personally overseeing my case and I think I shall be out in days to join you in planting those potatoes,' concluded Daauji.

> *alir bāṇo jyotiṣakaḥ*
> *stabdhībhūtaḥ kimekakaḥ*
> *preṣitā-preṣakaś caiva*
> *ṣaḍ ete sevakādhamāḥ*

Friends, as we have an interdependent existence, we always need each other's assistance to move forward in life. This interesting verse enlists six types of unsatisfactory assistants.

Alir: The first is compared to a bee (*alir*). In western culture, a hard worker is often referred to as a 'busy bee'. In this verse however, another temperament of the bee is implied, which refers to an unsatisfactory assistant. A person with a restless and fickle nature like that of a bee does not often carry the most dependable set of hands. Also, when one's interest in helping others is centred on their personal gain, such a mindset is undesirable. While the bee unknowingly helps in crop pollination, it willingly discards flowerless trees and even abandons flowers from which it has taken nectar. The bee's restlessness and gainful offers of help are being referred to in this verse as undesirable. When help is expected of us, we need to make sure that we value the people involved and not make helping others something we ourselves gain from, always.

Bāṇo: Second in the list is a foul-mouthed assistant referred to here as bāṇo. When asked to help, they shoot back words like piercing arrows. You think twice about seeking their help and turn to them only when there are no other alternatives available. Such people treat a call for collaboration as a spam call, often too self-absorbed in their own plans or relaxation. While helping others, our irritability, whether verbal or behavioural, puts us in this category. We should understand that we too need help from time to time and if we deem it right to extend some help to others, then why not do it in an amiable mood?

Jyotiṣaka: 'Oh yeah, that thing you wanted me to do . . . yeah, yeah, I'm on to it. I'll get it done tomorrow, promise. Just been busy all week.' The third of the undependable helpers are such procrastinators (*jyotiṣaka*). Agreeing to help but unwilling to keep their promise, they keep us guessing. Postponing things perpetually, they neither pull out of the matter nor put in the required effort. Let's not keep others hanging with the rope of hope and honour the confidence others have shown in us while seeking our assistance.

Stabdhībhūta: Fourth on the list of the undependable is the lazy couch potato (*stabdhībhūta*). Their laziness is not limited to physical lethargy, but also a mental attitude of laziness towards the needs of others. Many people turn this way when a regular contribution of effort is required from them. Often, the victims of their false promises are people closest to them—parents, children, flatmates, team mates, etc. Such persons inspire pending requests to be withdrawn without even mentioning it to them. To get over such a tendency in ourselves, we should develop appreciation for what others do for us without our asking or without even telling us. Thoughtful reciprocation is a sure cure for the indifference we may feel toward people's requests for help.

Kimekaka: This is an assistant who needs constant prodding and urging to get things done. They are like a machine that cannot operate autonomously and requires constant supervision. Weekly, daily or even hourly updates are required to get the task assigned to them completed. They are neither unwilling nor incapable of helping. In fact, they are often talented and agreeable. But either due to a lack of self-discipline or a lack of drive, their output is slow. To win over such a weakness in ourselves, we need to build momentum in what we do and enforce discipline in the execution of our plans.

Preṣita-preṣaka: The guy who is a master of excuses and king of delegating his responsibilities to others. When asked for help, they express an instant and over-the-top assurance of considering the work done. But their promises are more like lip service. They involve many others in the task expected from them and keep playing Chinese whispers instead of actually doing the needful. They keep passing the buck from one person to the other and keep assuring us that they are waiting for such and such person's contribution to get things completed at their end. Dealing with them can be time-costly and frustrating. Such tendencies can be corrected by avoiding taking on responsibilities beyond our capacity, avoiding promising to help simply to look good in others' eyes and by avoiding committing to help based on assumed assistance from others. Take what you can do yourself and then do it!

OVERCOMING OBSTACLES IN SERVICE

Service is meant to be the central feature of all relationships. Without service to each other, relationships remain stale. Daauji, although thrown in jail, was still able to serve his helpless father by getting his field tilled. Our love, appreciation, respect and responsibility should translate into practical service to others. When we put our relationship with others above our comfort, above our egos and above calculations for personal gain, then despite all sorts of challenges and constraints, we are in a position to achieve way more than expected.

One of the best examples of such an extraordinary assistant is Sri Hanuman from the epic, the Ramayana. Endowed with love for Lord Rama, Hanuman was able to understand the heart of his master and served proactively by pre-empting what was required beyond the call of duty. Hanuman's determination deepened by thinking about the feelings of distress his master experienced while searching for

His missing consort. With his mind energized by thoughts of pleasing his beloved Rama, Hanuman overcame the many temptations and obstacles on his path of service.

Hanuman's untiring eagerness and enthusiasm to help his beloved Rama empowered him with sharper intelligence to deal with conflict, a heightened tolerance towards personal discomfort and gave him greater strength to deal with obstacles. Keeping his purpose foremost, distractions in the form of personal comfort and glory could not deter him in his objectives.

When we adopt such a thoughtful mood to serve others, we not only win their hearts, but also resourcefully deal with the discouragement we may face. In conclusion, circumstances may define our situations, but should not determine our commitment to serve others.

THIRTY-SEVEN

Two Precious Jewels

Human Quality: Integrity

Arjun Singh was a farm owner who lived in Jaipur. Every morning, alongside hundreds of other people, he too would rush to attend the morning prayer service at the ancient Radha Govinda Temple erected centuries ago by the king of Jaipur. Kunwar, Arjun's teenage son, was into fast food and fast bikes. Kunwar was turning eighteen in a few weeks and Arjun was considering what to buy him as a gift.

'Kunwar, you cannot develop a friendship with a machine even if it has a 1000cc engine. A horse on the other hand is a very intelligent and exciting friend to have. They do not pollute the environment, take you flying like the wind and can help you keep fit and active as you engage in caring for them,' said Arjun, proposing to buy Kunwar a nice horse for his upcoming birthday. Kunwar loved the idea!

A few days later, Arjun came to Pradeep, a horse seller in a distant village and purchased a fine horse for Kunwar.

Upon returning, he directed Kunwar to bathe and groom the horse nicely. Delighted to have a new horse, as Kunwar removed the saddle off its back, he found a pouch and brought it to his father. Upon opening it, they found jewels inside.

Bucking with joy, the young jockey exclaimed, 'Jackpot! Jackpot, Dad! Jackpot!'

Arjun, however, remained calm and looking at the jewels in his palm, said, 'Son, this is truly a monumental occasion. We have something worth a lot and can gain tremendously from it.'

With their newfound fortune, Kunwar was already daydreaming about his own horse ranch and a lavish lifestyle. But Arjun re-sealed the pouch, zipped it in his jacket's top pocket and told Kunwar that he was going to return it.

'I purchased the horse for you, son, not these diamonds. It is my duty to return them to the seller.'

In utter disbelief, Kunwar interjected, 'But Dad, we've found these jewels on our horse. They are ours now . . .'

Arjun interrupted with defiance, '. . . No, son. Respect, victory and money earned dishonestly corrupts our conscience and hinders our abilities to truly develop.'

By late afternoon, Arjun was back at the horse seller's. Pradeep was erecting a canopy roof as a shade for some of his ponies.

'I think I may have got more than what I paid for,' said Arjun, explaining the purpose of his return. Confused, Pradeep looked unsure as to what Arjun meant. Taking the small pouch out, Arjun held it before its owner's face.

'Looks familiar?' he asked.

Aghast, Pradeep looked at the little green velvet bag with horror. His hands spontaneously searched his pockets as if the small pouch had been on him all this while. In a moment, Pradeep snatched his life savings from Arjun's hand.

'I was spending a lot of farewell time with Teja before I sold him to you. That horse was my favourite. I had secured this pouch under his saddle when I went on a land auction. I was expecting that I'd have to sell some of these diamonds if I got a good deal on the land for a new horse barn. I did not end up buying anything there, but upon returning, forgot to remove this jewel pouch from under Teja's saddle,' explained Pradeep.

'That horse is certainly priceless and these jewels did not add much to its value,' added Arjun.

'Noble Ram bless you! I'm so grateful. You deserve to be rewarded,' said Pradeep.

Arjun smiled respectfully.

'I must reward you. Who in today's world is so honest? Please accept a couple of jewels from my bag. I still can't believe that you have returned my life's fortune to me,' said the old man.

Declining the offer, Arjun said, 'I'm fine, thank you for your generous offer. You are such a gentleman.'

But Pradeep was in no mood to take Arjun's 'no' and persisted with his request.

'No son, you must be rewarded!'

'Actually, I have already kept a jewel with me. So, I don't need more,' said Arjun, conceding.

Dismayed, Pradeep immediately started counting the jewels within the bag. A few repeated counts later, he said, '. . . eighteen, nineteen, twenty. All twenty of the precious stones are here. Which jewel did you keep?'

'I have kept my jewel of integrity. I don't need to lose my permanent asset to gain a temporary one,' Arjun replied.

'It's an honour to know you. Your son is very fortunate to be raised by a father like you. Before you go, tell me honestly, were my jewels not at all able to tempt you?' the old man asked with a contented smile on his face.

'Temptations work on those who are starving. For a joyfully satisfied heart, the glamour of temptations does not work,' replied Arjun.

'Son, may I ask what the secret of your satisfaction and integrity is?' said Pradeep.

'Baba, I have been attending the morning aarti ceremony at Govind Devji temple in Jaipur for the last forty years . . . since I was a young child. I have a developed a relationship with the Lord. How would I face Him tomorrow morning after having robbed you of your life's savings? It would be shamefully hypocritical of me to claim to love God and, at the same time, cheat His children,' explained Arjun.

'How very wonderful! I see now who is behind your integrity to protect you from temptations. Your standard of morality is truly worth emulating,' said Pradeep, shaking hands with Arjun.

'Wealth gained at the expense of the wealth of relationships, especially our relationship with God, is a bad bargain. I do not want to be a rich man with an impoverished heart,' replied Arjun, while shaking Pradeep's hand.

'You are wise beyond your years. Why don't you stay for dinner and we can talk more,' proposed the old man.

'I have to excuse myself. Maybe another day. It's already late and I would like to return home. I do not want to miss my morning appointment with Govind Devji. I start my day early with the morning aarti ceremony at the temple. It keeps me internally well-oriented to deal with whatever fate may throw at me—jewels or rocks,' said Arjun modestly, laughing in jest.

'You long to see God and I am sure He longs to see you too!' said Pradeep, laughing in return.

'He longs to see each one of us and is always watching over us. Even when we are unaware or forgetful of this fact. His grace is always there. He was watching over you when you forgot to remove your jewels from that horse and He sent me to return to you what He has granted to you as yours. It is only His love for you, and it is only that same love that gives me the strength to turn away from temptations,' concluded Arjun, as Pradeep walked over and gave him a fatherly hug.

> *mātṛvat para-dāreṣu*
> *para-dravyeṣu loṣṭravat*
> *ātmavat sarva-bhūteṣu*
> *yaḥ paśyati sa paṇḍitaḥ*
> *Cāṇakya-śloka (10)*

Friends, this wisdom is from Chanakya Pandit, a great moralist and a genius in public affairs. Here, Chanakya is presenting a very wholesome definition of a truly learned man. He is suggesting that an educated person is to be identified not so much by his formal qualifications, degrees and certifications, but by his conduct and his vision towards the world.

Chanakya is explaining that there are three dimensions to a truly wise person's vision (*paśyati sa paṇḍitaḥ*):

Such a wise person is morally principled towards sources of pleasure (*mātṛvat para-dāreṣu*), like a man who sees another's wife as respectably as his own mother. The intelligence of such people is far stronger than their mental and sensual urges. Self-control, a feature of intelligence, is well-developed in them.

But how?

A wise person is incorruptibly trustworthy towards others' possessions (*para-dravyeṣu loṣṭravat*) since what does not belong to him appears unattractive to him, like undesirable junk. Arjun in this story was such a wise man. Such people assign higher non-monetary value to the real wealth of life.

But why?

Finally, such wise people are endowed with a spirit of equality towards fellow beings (*ātmavat sarva-bhūteṣu*), seeing all other beings as if they are themselves. They are sensitive and considerate of other people and feel happy in their happiness and pain in their suffering.

But on what basis does this work?

Let us answer these three questions based on time-tested yoga philosophy.

SPIRITUAL PERSPECTIVE THROUGH THE EYES OF WISDOM

The prevalent materialistic worldview, summarized in one hashtag—**#YOLO, Y**ou **O**nly **L**ive **O**nce—inadvertently invokes selfishness in us. Believing that we are here today and gone tomorrow, we have no reason to hold ourselves back from squeezing out whatever happiness we can, before our time runs out and we disappear forever. Selfishness and exploitative attitudes are often rooted in such spiritual amnesia.

Accountable to none, least of all to future generations, we exploit the planet and its people. Conflict becomes commonplace for control over the limited resources of enjoyment. In such a world, it is person against person, community against community, country against country. Everyone who is ill-informed about their own eternal spiritual nature is willing to fight it out for their happiness since, #YOLO.

In contrast, the worldview of Chanakya's 'wise man' has its foundation in spiritual wisdom. When we learn from authentic wisdom texts like the Gita, that in our core identity we all are souls, parts of the Supreme Lord, we learn that every sentient being is eternal, conscious and pleasure-seeking. As a result of such developed spiritual consciousness, we come to see how every sentient being is connected to others and shares the same essential joys and sorrows.

Materially, although each one of us is demographically different (physically, culturally, economically, etc.), through spiritual knowledge we get to learn how we all are spiritually equal. Such spiritual philosophy in practice garners in us a natural spirit of equality (*ātmavat sarva-bhūteṣu*). As a result, we live as more considerate, empathetic and socially responsible individuals.

AN INSIDE-OUT SOLUTION

The prevalent contemporary culture worships money, power and position. Unrestricted access to sensuality is the desired fruit of such worship. And for these devotees of materialism, ethics and morals become negotiable through subjective moral reasoning. Fanatic materialists and their blind followers do not even wish to consider the spiritual dimension. Their myopic view is concentrated on material enjoyment through advancement of material facilities. But the inner void created by the insufficiency of material pleasure leads only to frustration. Trying to escape reality through drugs, porn and alcohol then becomes a necessity.

The Bhagavad Gita explains that to remedy the external, we need to reorient the internal. Our need for happiness, which is essentially the spiritual appetite of the soul for the Supreme Soul, takes us to all lengths when we are ignorant of its spiritual basis. Self-control is elusive when we don't understand the 'self'. And as our own experience tells us, the brute force of abstinence is neither sufficient nor joyful to exercise self-control. Trust, promises, policies and even laws are broken as a result. But through spiritual wisdom, culture and practice, we are able to access higher spiritual pleasure in connection with God. The linking process of bhakti-yoga helps us find inner joy so profoundly elevating and grounding at the same time that to navigate through the world of temptations becomes not only possible, but easy.

THIRTY-EIGHT

When to Fight, When to Submit

Human Quality: Seeking Shelter

Five thousand years ago, the battle of Kurukshetra was in full swing. Untouched by fear, the valiant heroes on both sides knew there was zero margin for error in this encounter. Experts in combat, the heroes had deployed their regiments strategically to target the enemy side, look for loopholes and remain observant of booby-traps. With the ever-undefeated Bhishma and master strategist Yudhisthira, with pixel precision archers like Karana and Arjuna, and with brute force strikers like Duryodhana and Bheema, the contest seemed balanced between the two sides and destined for a timely and clear outcome.

Dhritrashtra, the blind but incumbent head of state, sat up nervously as his personal secretary Sanjay described to him the proceedings of the war.

From the southern end of the battlefield, finding his opportunity, the learned but nefarious Ashwathama unleashed a powerful weapon. Invoked in a state of meditation by a non-communicative sound wave, this was the Narayana Astra, a dynamic weapon. The weapon worked according to both the physical formation of the opponents' army and their mental state. The virtuous Pandavas were quickly realizing its increasing power.

As the Pandavas escalated their counterattack to neutralize the Narayana Astra, the mystical weapon increased in its fury, counter-neutralizing everything used against it. The war seemed to have reached a premature early end with the Pandava army quickly running out of options.

Earlier, Lord Krishna's benevolence towards even the demonic was seen when He personally went to Duryodhana to seek peace on the most accommodating terms. With all peace talks failing, Krishna had declared that since both sides were dear to Him, He would only have a non-combatant role in the inevitable war. Despite knowing this, Arjuna desired for Krishna to be his counsel and to drive his chariot in this fight for justice. Duryodhana, the war-hungry diplomat, had pounced on the opportunity to ask for Krishna's army to join his side. Krishna had impartially granted both of them their wishes. Though it seemed now, in the presence of the Narayana Astra, that neither of those choices was going to make any difference.

Hearing these descriptions gave joy to Dhritrashtra's heart. Although aware of the ignoble intentions and malevolent conduct of his sons that led to this fratricidal war, the prospect of usurping the throne was too big an incentive for the unrighteous blind king to let go. As his nephews, the Pandavas, the rightful owners of the land, were being overpowered by the Narayana Astra, Dhritrashtra's attachment to their kingdom was evident in his gleeful smile. But soon that smile began to disappear as Sanjay proceeded with his war commentary.

'Lord Krishna, Arjuna's charioteer, is signalling something to the Pandavas. What's this . . . the Pandavas are getting off their chariots and putting down the weapons they are holding in front of the Narayana Astra.'

'Have they surrendered, Sanjay? Are they accepting their defeat? Is this the end of the war? Tell me, Sanjay, say something!' spoke Dhritrashtra with his emotions raging in excitement.

'I don't understand, my lord. If that is the case and the Pandavas have accepted defeat, then why are the generals on your side not celebrating? Your beloved son, Prince Duryodhana looks especially dejected,' replied Sanjay.

'Have the Pandavas invoked any other weapons? Has the Narayana Astra fired its fury on them? Tell me everything you are envisioning,' petitioned Dhritrashtra.

'O king, it looks like Lord Krishna is guiding the Pandava camp on how to supplicate the Narayana Astra. The troops headed by the five Pandava brothers are engaging in glorifying Lord Narayana right in the middle of the battlefield,' explained Sanjay.

'The Narayana Astra never fails to complete the task for which it has been successfully invoked. It must burn down the entire Pandava army. What is Krishna doing now?' asked Dhritrashtra with visible frustration on his face.

'Krishna seems to be addressing everyone on the battlefield, not just the Pandavas,' Sanjay replied.

'What is He saying? Tell me everything . . .' Dhritrashtra petitioned again.

Sanjay repeated the words of Lord Krishna to Dhritrashtra:

'This omnipotent Narayana Astra is Lord Narayana's personal weapon and unlike all other weapons which are mechanical, chemical or astral, it is transcendental and omniscient like Him. Surrender, surrender in your body, words and mind to Lord Narayana. He's the benefactor and protector of all surrendered souls. Everyone belongs to Him. No one is His friend and no one is His enemy. He's like a wish-fulfilling tree. He grants what we sincerely desire from Him. He's impartial and His heart knows our heart. If we wish for Him to fight, He fights. If we wish to befriend Him, He's the first to accept us. Simply take shelter of Him and receive His boon.'

'Alas, we were on the verge of victory!' cried Dhritrashtra.

'O king, no one in your army is complaining, although they all look discouraged. Who can dispute with the supremely independent nature of Lord Narayana? Everybody seeks His favour, but not everybody is willing to surrender to Him,' said Sanjay.

'Lord Narayana is the friend of all. And He knows how I would love my sons to win. Why can't we get such assistance from Him, Sanjay?' said Dhritrashtra with desperation in his voice.

'O king, there is what the Lord allows us to do, but there is also what He expects us to do. When we breach the codes of righteousness, we become implicated with such misuse of our free will. Turning away from Him, we then act out the evil of our heart but are punished accordingly. But when we use our free will to uphold what is right, just and moral, then we are rewarded. Anyone can get the Lord's assistance by sincerely turning towards Him,' explained Sanjay.

'But wait, O king! What do I see now? That's Bheema, the commander-in-chief of the Pandava army. He has just arrived at the scene in his fast-drawn chariot. Is that him challenging the Narayana Astra?' Sanjay's excitement muzzled up with confusion.

'What is Bheema doing? Tell me, tell me now . . .' Dhritrashtra said with new excitement in his voice.

Sanjay repeated the words of Bheema:

'I, Bheemsen, the son of the great Pandu, cannot be dissuaded. Death on the battlefield is glorious for me. I am not going to bend my knees and be seen as a coward in front of my enemy's weapon. I'd rather die by the fury of the glorious Narayana Astra than give up the warrior ethos of kshatriya-dharma.'

Dhritrashtra jumped up, knowing well what Bheema's challenge meant and said, 'Yes! Now we are back into the contest. What is that Bheema doing now?'

Sanjay reported the scene, 'O king, true to the spirit of a kshatriya warrior, Bheema is readying himself for a one-to-one contest with the Narayana Astra. There is excitement in your camp.'

'The giant Bheema will be reduced to ashes and without their commander-in-chief, the Pandavas will crash like a pack of cards. We will soon be victorious! My Duryodhana's ascendency to the throne is clear now,' Dhritrashtra spoke in a self-congratulatory tone.

'But what's this, O king? Is that Lord Krishna jumping on Bheema? Unbelievable! Bheema, with the strength of 10,000 elephants, is the strongest wrestler in both the armies. But he is being tipped to the ground effortlessly by the tender looking Krishna,' reported Sanjay.

'Oh! Krishna again!' said Dhritrashtra in alarm as Sanjay repeated Krishna's words to him:

'Brother Bheema, before you fight it out, you have to first pay your respects to the Narayana Astra. I am only assisting you with what you have forgotten. This Narayana Astra cannot be commanded or defeated. It can only be invoked or pacified by calling it out of love and respect. That is the only language it understands. And I don't think you have any problem agreeing with me. Right, Bheema bhaiya?'

Hearing Krishna speak like this, Dhritrashtra lost his patience as Sanjay further explained to him what he saw.

'It seems that Lord Krishna has overpowered Bheema, who is not able to stand up. He is continuing to pay his respects to the Narayana Astra. Now Krishna is smiling at the Narayana Astra, which has bowed down to Him and has disappeared without harming anybody,' elaborated Sanjay.

'Krishna always comes to the rescue of His righteous devotees,' whispered Dhritrashtra to himself, silently accepting the supremacy of Krishna's protective love for His loving devotees, despite His impartiality towards everyone.

sarva-dharmān parityajya
mām ekaṁ śaraṇaṁ vraja
ahaṁ tvāṁ sarva-pāpebhyo
mokṣayiṣyāmi mā śucaḥ

Friends, this is often considered the *charam–shloka* or the highest/conclusive verse from the entire Vedic Hindu library. It appears in the eighteenth chapter of the Gita, the primeval book of spiritual knowledge on action, yoga, wisdom and love. It presents the culmination of all the yoga paths described by

Krishna to Arjuna; it also works as the underlying answer to all of life's dilemmas.

Having enlightened Arjuna on the various levels of what reality, duty and morality are, Krishna explains a framework to him in this chapter on how to best fulfil our specific duties towards the different realities of our subjective lives.

In the verse above (Bhagavad Gita 18.66), Krishna explains that in the highest reality, our duty and morality is for us to offer our love to the Divine and find shelter in Him.

Without such love and shelter, life's perplexities and perversities dishearten, overwhelm and provoke us time and again. Broken emotionally as a result, we respond to problems in self-implicating ways. This often generates feelings of confusion, resentment, loneliness and self-hate, and it expands a burning void of sorrow inside us. Self-doubt then creeps in and saps our fighting spirit. This is exactly what happened to Arjuna at the start of the Gita when he tried to handle his challenges alone, disconnected from the Supreme will.

But as this verse presents, invoking the shelter of the Supreme Being by lovingly reaching out to Him enables us to tap into a reality far grander than our immediate obstacles and reversals. Perceiving our small but significant place in that bigger picture and reconnected with the Supreme, uplifts us beyond unnecessary worries. It breaks the wall of illusion that prevents God's reciprocal love to reach us and naturally gets rid of our depression and loneliness. Realizing that we are not alone in our struggles lightens our burden. Enriched with divine care, our hearts feel empowered to put up an honest fight against life's reversals and grants us clarity on when to let go.

FINDING SHELTER AND LETTING GO—SIGNS OF WEAKNESS?

Undesired disagreements, unpredictable layoffs, financial volatility and climate catastrophes are some common scenarios beyond our control. When we run into problems beyond our power to respond, is it wise to continue the fight, like Bheema against the Narayana Astra? Or do we allow ourselves to be either overwhelmed like a prey animal or get hurt while fighting a losing battle? Who do we turn to when nobody is able to help our situation?

This verse explains that things out of our control are still under the control of God. But some people perceive taking shelter in God as anti-intellectual, as an abandonment of intelligence and a sign of weakness. They draw nihilistic conclusions in the face of such suffering; life and this world appear meaningless to such thinkers. But when we take shelter in a truth far greater than ourselves, we find both help and meaning, even in the face of such suffering.

Through spiritual wisdom, we learn that we are indestructible souls and that God is always with us. Knowing our eternality empowers us and we feel peace and strength to calmly discern a way ahead. This inspires us to fully engage our God-given skills to focus on things that are in our control and let go of the things that are not. With God's grace behind us, we are able to deal with the inevitable suffering of our material existence. We understand that suffering is not retributive punishment from a sadistic god, but a course of restorative development for our inner development. It enables us to overcome our weaknesses that mislead our will and implicate us with the avoidable distresses and habits that choke our potential.

But beyond the utilitarian benefits mentioned above, this verse reveals the most comforting truth, that we are never alone and that our need for ever-increasing love is legitimate. We only need turn to the shelter of God from where we are to find that love.

THIRTY-NINE

Move from Comfort Zone to Effort Zone

Human Quality: Equality

Jaanaki Kishori was the daughter of a cobbler. Coming from a very poor family, Jaanaki could not afford to attend school. She taught herself to read with the help of Sumitra, the local priest's wife. Despite financial and social disadvantages, Jaanaki was dexterous and determined. At the behest of the priest, some local students lent Jaanaki their previous year's course material since she could not afford to buy the books. In this way, while helping her father mend shoes during the day, Jaanaki studied under the street light outside her hut during the evenings.

With the help of a pious businessman, the priest secured funds for Jaanaki to attend year ten at school. Truly talented, Jaanaki won a full scholarship to college, scoring the highest marks in the district for her matriculation exam. During the first weeks at college, Jaanaki faced bullying at the hands of many seniors.

'College life is full of prejudices and judgements. I am being singled out for my looks, poverty and for being the daughter of a cobbler,' complained Jaanaki to the priest and his family as they sat in their small living room.

'Have you forgotten all that I have taught you from the Gita, Jaanaki? You are not black or white, tall or short, lean or fat. You are not your clothes or your shoes. You are neither your looks nor your hairstyle. Remember, you are a spiritual spark, an emanation from the supremely beautiful Lord who is the father of everyone. The body is as much a dress of the soul as are the clothes you are being bullied for. The body is ageing and will ultimately wither away like an old dress, however expensive it may be perceived today. But the soul, the real person residing in the body is eternal and far beyond its mundane identities. If you work without this spiritual knowledge, you will continue the suffering-cycle of birth and death whether rich or poor,' said the priest.

Jaanaki heard him patiently, but quietly looked skywards.

'My dear daughter, rise above these bodily superficialities. Otherwise, consumed by such externalities, you will miss your golden opportunity of human life. My child, you are not your body, financial status, social hierarchy or any other bodily designation,' said the priest as Sumitra held Jaanaki's hand in between hers.

But Jaanaki responded in a resentful tone, 'I remember all this Prabhu ji, but I want to give a befitting reply to their harsh words and shut them up once and for all.'

The priest's elder daughter Yamuna then came and sat in front of Jaanaki on the chair opposite hers and spoke to her like an elder sister trying to dissuade her younger sibling from doing something harmful.

'Kishori, you are my inspiration in life. Remember the poem you wrote for my school recital many years ago? I always read it when I feel low. It always uplifts me. I have it here. Let me read it to you, my little sister. It will serve as a great reminder of what we stand for in life.' Saying thus, the priest's daughter took out a piece of paper and read out loud:

DREAMING REALITY BY JAANAKI KISHORI

If life is just a passing dream,
Then what are those that I dream at night?
And what about those I see with open eyes?
Probably they are little sparks,
In a speck of flame.
Both are there,
One inside the other.
Just a matter of time,
They are there,
But of course ending,
Both are dying.
As a flash of light they say,
Your whole life is played,
Again at the time,
When time stops on you.
Death they name it,
The End,
No More.
How silly!
Indeed it's a new start,
When yours is left behind,
But you move on.
To a new dream,
To dream more dreams,

To claim new me and mine,
But the same old,
Yet ever-new,
The eternal soul,
The essence,
The same 'I'.
Dreams are all but imagination,
Speculation,
Anticipation of all categorized as desires,
It needs correction,
Projection in a new direction.
For the insatiable desires to reach perfection,
That is to say, complete satisfaction.
But in dreams is it possible?
I doubt.
So, let the dreams end!
And reality begin.
Where there are no more false connections,
Where life is not a passing dream,
A once-upon-a-time story.
But the eternity,
On the other side of salvation,
Where darkness ends,
With trance and illumination.
For that reality,
I shall dream.
With these sleepless eyes,
Need to want some rest,
From this endless journey.
Soon enough before this dream ends,

Shall I prepare to open my eyes.
Dream shall I no more,
Reality for all I seek.

'Wow, you wrote this, Jaanaki?' asked the priest.

'Yes, I wrote this based on your Gita lessons at the temple,' she replied.

'I am so proud of you,' said Yamuna.

'Yes, I am also very proud of my Kishori. With this wisdom of the Gita in you, I am a little surprised that you are taking their ignorance about the real you so seriously. Be confident the way the Lord has made you, my child. You are His prized creation. A spark of His splendour shines in you. You are lovely the way the Lord has fashioned you. He has given you uniquely special features. You won't get anywhere by valuing the false opinions of others about you. You have no control over these external things or what others say about you. Beneath our poor body resides our priceless soul. We are rich or poor by what we hold on to . . . the body or the soul?' said Sumitra as she cleared away the tears that had swelled up in the poor girl's eyes.

Jaanaki understood that the priest's family was trying to show her the spiritual perspective to help her deal with her inescapable material reality.

'My child, do not get distracted by what others say. I can see how you are being dragged down to low level thinking. I'm afraid you will only end up becoming a copy of what you despise if you get caught up with their narratives. Instead, focus on your real assets and utilize your God-given gifts to make a positive contribution. Then you will experience real happiness in life,' concluded Sumitra.

'Thank you Maa and Prabhu ji. Thank you, Yamuna didi. I truly appreciate your support. I guess my retaliation was a reaction of my feeling attacked and hurt,' said Jaanaki with a sense of relief in her voice.

'Daughter, know that others cannot hurt you unless you allow them. There is no gain venting extraordinarily and wasting time hyperventilating about thoughtless egoism. By criticizing others, you may find temporary relief, but it will not change what is not in your control. Do not reduce your identity to your looks or your socio-economic status. Focus on your inner growth and development,' said the priest, smiling reassuringly.

With the help of the priest's family, Jaanaki reoriented herself and despite the mocking and the bullying, remained focused and did not implicate herself in useless fights and arguments at college. Her resilience paid off when she earned everyone's respect by scoring the highest marks ever scored by a first-year student. And thanks to her helpful and generous nature, she won many sincere friendships.

Time moved on and, encouraged by her professors, Jaanaki stood for the post of the president of the college's student council. Using her vast spiritual knowledge, she scripted speeches that spoke of her inclusive vision and selfless dedication. Her strong oratory skills gave goosebumps even to attendees from rival groups. Crossing one hurdle at a time, Jaanaki won the top seat in the college elections. Her rival Rajdeep could only get one-third of the vote share.

At the first public address by the newly elected president of the student council, Jaanaki Kishori entered the college auditorium to a big welcome cheer. There was excitement in everyone's heart. Rajdeep, however, turned out to be a sore loser. He stationed himself along with his gang in the first row of seats. As Jaanaki, dressed in a simple white saree with a red border, climbed the stage to speak, some of the girls in the rival group made some unsavoury comments about her dress. Unaffected by the rude joke, Jaanaki smiled at everyone and thanked them for coming.

Before she could begin her inaugural speech, a young lady from Rajdeep's group, dressed in fashionable clothes and while still sitting, said loudly:

'Kishori, don't forget where you come from. You may have won an election, but it does not change anything about you.'

The whole group started laughing loudly. The plan was to embarrass Jaanaki and reduce her stature by publicly ridiculing her. Most other students felt uneasy and some even voiced their protestations.

Unfazed, Jaanaki first requested her supporters to calm down and then looked at her detractor. Replying with humility, she said, 'Yes Shipra, how can I begin without acknowledging my roots? Thank you for reminding me. Friends, I was born in a straw hut, but have accepted the whole world as my home, Vasudhaiva Kutumbakam.'

The auditorium thundered with loud applause.

Undeterred, another obnoxious young lady from the group stood up and said, 'Don't ever forget that your father used to make shoes for our families.'

Again, the entire gang burst into loud laughter.

Nodding her head in agreement, Jaanaki replied, 'Well, thank you for reminding me about my father. He raised me with dignity and values. I am very proud of the fact that my father makes and mends your shoes. He is a great cobbler and I am sure many here have had their shoes made by my daddy. He loves what he does and puts his heart into every pair of shoes he stitches. May I request you not to heckle any more? We all have gathered here for a purpose and have a busy day scheduled ahead. So let's move on . . .'

Seeing this kind of low behaviour, the hall grew impatient and the professors indignant. As one last attempt to emotionally scar her and break her down, one silly young man persisted with the public ridicule.

'Your father repaired my shoe last week, but it has broken open at the side again. He isn't such a great cobbler after all!'

With an honest expression on her face and with her head held high, Jaanaki immediately responded, 'My dear brother, I too am trained in making shoes. I would happily repair it for you. Please let us proceed now in the interest of time. I promise I will have a look at your shoe after this event. Is that ok?'

Her earnest appeal and goodwill finally broke through her detractor who looked stunned by the humility of their newly elected president. He sat down embarrassed with his face lowered in shame.

Before Rajdeep and her gang could disrupt the proceedings any further, a professor scolded them and escorted them out of the auditorium.

'Friends, this reminds me of what my guru taught me from the sixteenth chapter of the Gita. It is explained there that some people are so poor that all they have is money. While we cannot give anything to such poorly rich, we should not hesitate to forgive them for their poverty of heart,' said Jaanaki as the crowd rose up, applauding for a long while.

vidyā-vinaya-sampanne
brāhmaṇe gavi hastini
śuni caiva śva-pāke ca
paṇḍitāḥ sama-darśinaḥ

Friends, this is a verse from the fifth chapter of the Gita. It explains that, enlightened by the virtue of spiritual knowledge, we develop a sense of true equality towards the world.

How? With genuine spiritual growth, our vision of others evolves. We are thus able to recognize the spiritual equality of all beyond the obvious external material differences like physical, intellectual, social, cultural, economic and other similar parameters associated with our bodies, even religious ones.

The verse tells how the learned sees equality everywhere: in the teacher, the cow, the elephant, the dog and even the dog-eater.

Discrimination towards our fellow humans is disgraceful. While equality is a cherished value of human society, where is the equality in the obvious difference between a man and a cow mentioned in this verse? Yoga wisdom explains that it lies in the spiritual sameness of the soul in all beings. A basic fundamental of yoga wisdom is that all living beings—humans and non-humans—are non-material, spiritual beings, parts of the Supreme Spiritual Being and so, qualitatively equal. In our spiritual constitution, we all are unique individuals, neither superior nor inferior to each other.

EXCLUSIVE EQUALITY!

'All animals are equal, but some animals are more equal than others,' wrote George Orwell in his famous novella *Animal Farm*. Here, he is pointing out to the hypocrisy of systems that proclaim absolute equality of all, but give power and privileges to small groups of the elite. Is true equality really possible? Yes, but not at the material level.

Consider various parameters often used for measuring people at schools, colleges, competitive exams, interviews, loan offices, banks, hospitals, professional institutions, sporting events, etc. Height, weight, strength, age, GPA, test-ranking, IQ, EQ, credit history score—whatever material metrics we may use clearly show that people come out unequal. Therefore, the Gita declares that our social positions are determined by our qualities and our activities, not discriminatory deviations like caste systems or group identities based on our birth circumstances.

As history shows us, politics is played around our material differences whether racial, social or financial. It is one group against the other. The harmful effects of inequality must be countered. But a materialistic response to such injustice and inequality is often fought on the wrong premise.

MATERIAL VARIETY AND SPIRITUAL EQUALITY

Different people have different strengths and can contribute differently to society. Equality does not appear visible on the material plane. Material consideration always points out how people are different, not equal. But intuitively, we feel that everyone should be treated equally. Why?

Yoga texts explain that our intuition for equality is rooted in the spiritual sameness we share with everyone else. As parts of the Divine, we are similar in our core characteristics; we are eternal, conscious and pleasure-seeking.

Understanding of our common spiritual essence fosters empathy, promotes social harmony and engenders compassion towards all living beings.

In the benign aspiration for equality, people sometimes try to turn blind to the diversity of individuals, artificially denying all differences that conventionally create rigid walls in society. But often, such differences are very much a part of people's individual realities. By failing to acknowledge the real spiritual basis of our equality, we end up creating more factions, making the same mistake as those who we are dissenting against. As a result, we end up further from our sacred dream of equality.

FORTY

Who Can Escape the Chase?

Human Quality: Humaneness

The mystical and alluring Sundarbans forest ranges of West Bengal house many rare bird species and other wild wonders of nature. The island of Gosaba, the biggest inhabited island in the Sundarbans, hosts many cowherds, farmers and foresters. The foresters who live here subsist by trading forest resources like latex, gums, essential oils and medicinal plants. Wild animals like tigers, rhinoceros, barasingha and wild cats are always the worry of the people who live there. The cowherds especially are also always worried about the loss of their cattle to the jungle beasts. Surabhi was a beautiful Swarna-kapila Gir cow of a cowherd who lived near the island of Gosaba.

Once, while grazing, Surabhi lost her path and walked into the denser part of the forest. This part was ruled by Tygro, a magnificent Royal Bengal tiger. Oblivious to the presence of Tygro, Surabhi kept walking, munching on untouched soft grasses. Smelling the presence of a cow, Tygro jumped out of his cave and followed the navigation radar of his nose.

Approaching Surabhi from behind, Tygro stepped on a tree bark with his big and heavy paw and it made a loud crackling sound. Surabhi realized that she was under attack by a wild animal. With her survival instincts kicking in, she immediately started running towards the mainland. Tygro leapt into chase. A life and death contest ensued.

Running through the different parts of the forest, Surabhi bravely evaded the tiger's reach. With his eyes fixed on his prey, Tygro made wild noises as he closed in on Surabhi. Desperate to save her life, Surabhi jumped into a small pond that separated one part of the forest mangrove from another. Tygro too, in the heat of the chase, mindlessly jumped right behind her. Unfortunately, the pond was not as harmless as it looked; it was more like a pit of quicksand. The scene was that of helplessness with both the cow and the tiger stuck a short distance from each other. Overnight, both animals would be digested by this forest quicksand.

Frustrated and angry, Tygro growled:

'I can't wait to sink my claws in your skin and grab the back of your neck in my jaws. I will then pull you out of this silly pond and eat you slowly.'

But Tygro's strength and weight were acting against his claims. The more he tried to move closer to Surabhi, the more the quicksand pulled him down.

Stuck apart from her attacker, Surabhi's fear subsided. She replied with patience.

'We are both stuck here helplessly. The predator has turned into a prey.'

Angered by her words, Tygro growled, 'You silly cow! You wait and watch how I make music out of crunching your bones.'

Unscathed, Surabhi replied, 'A drowning man should become humble and ask for help, but drowned in your arrogance, you seem to be disconnected from ground reality.'

Irked even more, Tygro replied, 'I am gathering my breath from the chase. I will free myself shortly. Then I will pull myself out of this pit, though not alone, but with you in my jaws.'

Surabhi replied, 'Our freedom is not in our hands here. You continue to live in a self-imposed fiction induced by the strength you possessed in a different environment. Your past glory doesn't seem to leave you an option to consider your present handicaps.'

Even without a prospect of saving himself, Tygro's sadism painted grotesque pictures of violence towards his equally helpless co-victim of the quicksand.

Breaking an abrupt silence, Surabhi asked Tygro in a thoughtful tone, 'Hey, do you have a master?'

Annoyed, Tygro said, 'You silly bovine, how dare you insult me with a question like that. I am the king of this jungle. I'm the master of myself!'

'O king of the jungle, what power are you able to exercise now? All your strength and skills are null and void here. You can helplessly wait till time sinks you,' said Surabhi.

'Enough of your . . . stop talking from a pedestal,' retorted an angry Tygro.

'I am going to drown, but what about you? You are going to drown too!' added Tygro.

Smiling gently, Surabhi replied, 'No, I am not!'

'Oh, is that so . . . may I ask how you are going to free yourself from this quicksand?' snapped Tygro.

In a boastful tone, Tygro continued, 'I have hunted down an adult rhinoceros. Before I killed Teja, my rival in the forest, we both brought down a wild elephant. Now I have tried with all my might to free myself, but could not move an inch. How on earth are you going to step out of this pit of death?'

Patiently, Surabhi replied, 'I admit, I cannot free myself from this embrace of mud. But unlike you, I have a master. And while I cannot free myself, he can.'

Continuing with great confidence, Surabhi explained, 'When I do not reach home by the evening, finding me missing my master will come searching for me. He will definitely look for me in this part of the jungle known to have devoured many a buffalo. Once he finds me, he will raise me and escort me home.'

Tygro went silent and looked at Surabhi with disdainfully cold eyes.

Sure enough, as the sun set, Surabhi could hear a buffalo horn bugle blowing distantly, followed by calls of her name. In response, Surabhi mooed loudly with all her remaining strength. A little while later, Surabhi's master reached the site along with his two sons, who were holding long candle-wax flambeaus in their hands.

The three men unscrewed the burning ends of their fire torches connected to their long wooden handles. They carefully hung the burning ends on the tree branches and prepared to reach their trapped cow using these long wooden handles. Lifting Surabhi up and placing a wooden plank near her feet to support her, the herdsmen skilfully used their basic rescue tools. Once Surabhi was lifted enough, they threw a rope lasso around her body and lifted her out of the pit.

Once outside, the master fed the tired cow jaggery pieces to give her strength and both felt renewed gratitude for one another. Tygro did not mellow down and kept growling aggressively, putting fear in their hearts.

'Boys, this poor tiger is also a soul like us, now in a tiger's body. I dread the thought of one of us drowning in jungle quicksand. Let us do something to help it,' said the elderly master of Surabhi.

'But father, rescuing this beast puts our lives and the lives of many cows in danger. Just listen to his aggressive growls,' said his younger son.

'My boy, the tiger is acting as per the nature endowed by God on it. It only attacks for food. When man infringes its forest, where else would it find its habitat and food? For its power, we shall show it the respect it deserves, but we have to be careful not to deny it what we'd want for ourselves as a soul in need. Leaving it to drown here while we can help it will make us guilty in God's judgement,' replied the wise cowherd.

The cowherds decided not to rescue the tiger themselves and to bring the forest rangers to the spot the next morning. But by placing wooden planks under the tiger's body and tying the planks with ropes to tree branches overhead, they ensured Tygro wouldn't drown overnight. Thus they bought him time while a rescue operation could be coordinated the next morning.

Before walking away with her master, Surabhi looked at Tygro and spoke to him in animal language one last time.

'I think my master was talking about saving you. They are very loving and capable men. They would have saved you here and now if only you would have calmed down. Maybe they could have put you outside this pit for you to slowly recover your strength and leave without harming anyone. But I think your attitude scared them off. Sometimes it is wise to allow others to help you rather than dwelling in your own arrogance. Don't act so tough and make things difficult for yourself if they bring other farmers to rescue you tomorrow.'

Tygro could only stare at Surabhi along with her three guardians as they happily walked away towards their home. Next morning, Tygro was rescued and released deep into the forest by the efforts of the cowherds and forest rangers. By now he had understood the place of humility in character and the shelter of having a guardian in life.

na paśyati ca janmāndhaḥ kāmāndho naiva paśyati
na paśyati madonmattaḥ svārthī doṣānna paśyati

Friends, this verse from Cäëakya Néti reveals to us the different levels of blindness.

Janmāndhaḥ: Firstly, there are those who are born blind (*janmāndhaḥ*). Their physical blindness may hamper their abilities, but cannot stop them from making positive contributions with their life. In that sense, they are simply differently-abled and are the least of the blind.

Kāmāndho: Next are those who are blinded by lust (*kāmāndho*). Driven by lust, they often see people as objects for their gratification. The urge for pleasure blinds them to moral principles and even common decency. The veneer of excessive desire for material enjoyment (*kāma*) also turns people blind to what is fair and what is beneficial. Blinded by desires for material enjoyment, they end up hurting and harming others, themselves and even the environment.

Madonmattaḥ: Then there are those who are blinded due to intoxication caused by pride (*madonmattaḥ*). Their arrogance blinds them to their own inadequacies and limitations. And so they continue to believe that they are the best, the only repository of wisdom and abilities. They feel convinced that they know what they are doing and turn their backs to even the good advice of their well-wishers. Arrogance turns them to excuses or scapegoats in the face of failure, instead of seeking help for self-improvement.

Svārthī: Finally, the worst of the blind are those who due to selfishness are unable to see the fault in their self-centred priorities. Since they cannot see beyond their own needs and wants, they do not hesitate to treat others as disposable objects. They are blind to how their selfishness devours their morality and even humanity.

UNHELPFUL ATTITUDES, HELPFUL PERSPECTIVES

Friends, Tygro was blinded by pride and thought he needed nobody's help. His arrogance could have cost him his life were it not for the goodwill of the cowherds. Such is the nature of arrogance; it places us as the king or queen of an imaginary castle built by our opinions of ourselves. It then judges others as below us and makes us selective of who deserves our attention, respect, friendship or even an opportunity to help us.

Our condescending ego distances us from even our well-wishers and we end up lonely at the top, even if sitting on a real castle of worldly success.

Yoga wisdom explains that, as individual spiritual beings endowed with consciousness, we are eternal dependent parts of a whole far bigger than ourselves. By acknowledging that we are parts and not the whole, our feet can remain grounded in the anchor of humility preventing us from floating in imaginary glory. Further, when we see others as parts of the same whole, we come to respect them as unique equals, perhaps gifted differently than ourselves.

A part of the machine is most useful when it is connected with the machine and works alongside all other parts for a useful outcome. Similarly, when we come to learn of our common spiritual nature and same spiritual source, we can rise above our material advantages and disadvantages to lead a more cohesive life in sync with each other and our common source, God.

REVIVING HUMANITY THROUGH SPIRITUALITY

We set ourselves for a whole lot of unhealthy outcomes by denying our own eternal spirituality and taking ourselves as a temporary bag of biochemicals running a 'marvellous machine made of meat'.

Firstly, if we are just temporary machines, we inadvertently define our self-worth based on what we can do, since that's how machines are defined. People with fewer talents, contribution and output are not inferior beings, like primitive tools, as such a materialistic worldview would conclude or have them believe.

Secondly, if we are just slowly expiring creatures of material evolution, then what holds us back from procuring all that we can for our pleasure before our time runs out and we disappear forever?

Materialists propose that we are all here due to material evolution with neural functions in the brain disguised as our 'feelings'. They advocate the oneness of our human experience as the basis for our equality. But such an equality of experience does not define the experiencer in concrete terms. The reductionist view concludes that the very concept of the self or experiencer is an illusion and that we are simply a bunch of atoms temporarily providing a unified experience as a being and as a species. An equality based on the neural bombardment of atoms can only sum up to sentimental oneness and other forms of discrimination as is seen played against other sentient beings like farm animals, chickens, lambs, fish, etc.

But by learning about our real spiritual self and adopting powerful practices of processes like bhakti-yoga, we can come to realize our individual spiritual nature that we share with every sentient being, not just humans. We can then aspire to live a life of harmony with each other based on a far more concrete basis of our universal equality. Working towards the common purpose of reviving our dormant loving bond with our creator, we can live to contribute in this world in a mood of loving service to Him and His entire creation.

Acknowledgements

I wish to express my heartfelt gratitude to many wonderful souls who were part of the exciting journey of making this book happen, especially the wisdom and the lessons part of every story.

My gratitude to His Divine Grace Srila A.C. Bhaktivedanta Swami Prabhupada, the Founder Acharya of the International Society for Krishna Consciousness (ISKCON) for publishing the essence of the Vedic literatures—the Srimad Bhagavad Gita and the *Srimad Bhagavatam* published by the Bhaktivedanta Book Trust International (BBT) in multiple languages—thus making the ancient Vedic wisdom accessible to all.

My gratitude to His Holiness (H.H.) Radhanath Swami Maharaja for his personal guidance and training for nearly three decades and for facilitating my connection with Srila Prabhupada and ISKCON.

My heartfelt respects to H.H. Bhakti Rasamrita Swami Maharaja for introducing the concepts of the *Bhagavad Gita* to me in my student days.

My gratitude to my father A.K. Sitaraman (Achyut Jagannatha Das) and my mother Kalpakam Sitaraman (Sri Sachidevi Dasi) for nurturing my life with many spiritual wisdom stories and an excellent example of a stable emotionally warm family, which created the foundation for absorbing the teachings of Vedic Sanatana Dharma.

I wish to offer my loving respects and feelings of gratitude to my senior leaders in ISKCON who have been the source of inspiration for me to live life following the teachings of *Srimad Bhagavatam* and share stories of spiritual lessons with the world:

H.H. Gopal Krishna Goswami Maharaja, H.H. Jayapataka Swami Maharaja, H.H. Bhakticharu Swami Maharaja, H.H. Bhanu Swami Maharaja, H.H. Niranjana Swami Maharaja, H.H. Badrinarayana Swami Maharaja, H.H. Radhagovinda Goswami Maharaja, H.H. Sivarama Swami Maharaja, H.H. Bhaktitirtha Swami Maharaja, H.H. Tamal Krishna Goswami Maharaja, H.H. Satswaroopa Das Goswami Maharaja, Bhurijana Prabhu, Shyamasundar Prabhu and many other disciples of Srila Prabhupada.

I acknowledge the wisdom I gained from many in the ashram including Govinda Prabhu, Radhagopinatha Prabhu, Shyamananda Prabhu, Sanatkumar Prabhu, Radheshyam Prabhu and Sankirtan Prabhu.

I have been highly inspired by the books, lectures and association of Shikshashtakam Prabhu, Gaur Gopal Prabhu, Vrajavihari Prabhu, Chaitanya Charan Prabhu, Shubh Vilas Prabhu and Sutapa Prabhu and acknowledge my gratitude to them for igniting many inspiring thoughts in me.

My special thanks to Suhail Mathur of The Book Bakers and Gurveen Chadha of Penguin Random House for their patient and expert guidance and intervention to craft the final version of the book.

My gratitude to the team of Ananda Caitanya Prabhu, Dr Sumanta Rudra, Gauranga Darshan Prabhu and the BRC team for their support and help.

My gratitude to Gaurava Sharma for his diligent work on every aspect of the book taking its final shape. Special thanks to Vinay Raniga and Vrushali Potnis Damle for their help with proofreading and editing.